A Louisiana Gentleman

by Rosary Hartel O'Neill

A Samuel French Acting Edition

Founded 1830
New York Hollywood London Toronto
SAMUELFRENCH.COM

Copyright © 2008, 2010 by Rosary Hartel O'Neill

ALL RIGHTS RESERVED

CAUTION: Professionals and amateurs are hereby warned that *A LOUISIANA GENTLEMAN* is subject to a Licensing Fee. It is fully protected under the copyright laws of the United States of America, the British Commonwealth, including Canada, and all other countries of the Copyright Union. All rights, including professional, amateur, motion picture, recitation, lecturing, public reading, radio broadcasting, television and the rights of translation into foreign languages are strictly reserved. In its present form the play is dedicated to the reading public only.

The amateur live stage performance rights to *A LOUISIANA GENTLEMAN* are controlled exclusively by Samuel French, Inc., and licensing arrangements and performance licenses must be secured well in advance of presentation. PLEASE NOTE that amateur Licensing Fees are set upon application in accordance with your producing circumstances. When applying for a licensing quotation and a performance license please give us the number of performances intended, dates of production, your seating capacity and admission fee. Licensing Fees are payable one week before the opening performance of the play to Samuel French, Inc., at 45 W. 25th Street, New York, NY 10010.

Licensing Fee of the required amount must be paid whether the play is presented for charity or gain and whether or not admission is charged.

Stock licensing fees quoted upon application to Samuel French, Inc.

For all other rights than those stipulated above, apply to: The Marton Agency, 1 Union Square, Suite 815, New York, NY 10003; Info@MartonAgency.com.

Particular emphasis is laid on the question of amateur or professional readings, permission and terms for which must be secured in writing from Samuel French, Inc.

Copying from this book in whole or in part is strictly forbidden by law, and the right of performance is not transferable.

Whenever the play is produced the following notice must appear on all programs, printing and advertising for the play: "Produced by special arrangement with Samuel French, Inc."

Due authorship credit must be given on all programs, printing and advertising for the play.

ISBN 978-0-573-69765-4

No one shall commit or authorize any act or omission by which the copyright of, or the right to copyright, this play may be impaired.

No one shall make any changes in this play for the purpose of production.

Publication of this play does not imply availability for performance. Both amateurs and professionals considering a production are strongly advised in their own interests to apply to Samuel French, Inc., for written permission before starting rehearsals, advertising, or booking a theatre.

No part of this book may be reproduced, stored in a retrieval system, or transmitted in any form, by any means, now known or yet to be invented, including mechanical, electronic, photocopying, recording, videotaping, or otherwise, without the prior written permission of the publisher.

MUSIC USE NOTE

Licensees are solely responsible for obtaining formal written permission from copyright owners to use copyrighted music in the performance of this play and are strongly cautioned to do so. If no such permission is obtained by the licensee, then the licensee must use only original music that the licensee owns and controls. Licensees are solely responsible and liable for all music clearances and shall indemnify the copyright owners of the play and their licensing agent, Samuel French, Inc., against any costs, expenses, losses and liabilities arising from the use of music by licensees.

IMPORTANT BILLING AND CREDIT REQUIREMENTS

All producers of *A LOUISIANA GENTLEMAN* must give credit to the Author of the Play in all programs distributed in connection with performances of the Play, and in all instances in which the title of the Play appears for the purposes of advertising, publicizing or otherwise exploiting the Play and/or a production. The name of the Author *must* appear on a separate line on which no other name appears, immediately following the title and *must* appear in size of type not less than fifty percent of the size of the title type.

A LOUISANA GENTLEMAN was originally performed at Théâtre de Nesle, Paris, France and Brotfabrik Theatre, Bonn, Germany

CHARACTERS

BLAINE ASHTON: A kind young man, 24, who is attempting to sculpt a happy life for himself, despite the women around him who are hungry for his strength.

GILLIAN PEDERSON-KRAG: A 36 year-old actress. Seductive, talented. Her beauty and style evoke jealousy in others. She pushes herself to extremes to gain acceptance from those she loves.

DALE ELLEN ASHTON: BLAINE'S 16 year-old sister. She has a haunted radiance that makes her fragility more precious. Like a butterfly, her short life is all the more beautiful. She has lost her father and is trying to tap into her psychic power.

SARA AIMÉE BIRDSONG: 45-65, the aunt. **SARA** jealously guards her reputation as the most glamorous woman in New Orleans. She doesn't know how to survive without a man to take care of her.

SETTING

BLAINE ASHTON'S apartment in Baroness Micaela de Pontalba's Buildings, the French Quarter, New Orleans. The apartment fronts the old heart of the city—Jackson Square, the Cabildo Museum, the Saint Louis Cathedral, and the Presbytere—shrines now molding in the humid air from the Mississippi River. With their high ceilings, tall windows, and brick, the apartments remind one of the *Palais Royal,* the Parisian buildings that inspired them. Giant furnishings bleached by the sun—a chaise lounge, an armoire, an oriental carpet of raspberry and cream—lend the room a mythic poignancy. The apartment seems to scream "If I had to do it over again, I would prioritize extravagance." And this selfishness is seen in the slightly empty feeling that surrounds the effigies to the past, the statues, the portraits of family members with their smiles of deceit. Over the mantle, a portrait of Dr. James Ashton lords over the marble busts of his children, Blaine and Dale, below.

The set contains an area for a balcony, a living area and a bedroom. The architecture is barely suggested. All three areas form a harmonious whole, like a complete scene rather than disparate ones. A dreamlike timeless present mood should result from an emphasis on motion and the expanse of lavender sky encircling the apartment. The sequence of scenes should have a whole, flowing feeling and changes of time should be accomplished by changes of lighting.

TIME

The present. It is twilight, that uncertain time between the quiet of night and the noise of day when the apartments blend into the shadows. Lost characters drift out on the streets, joining the tourists with their throwaway cameras and the homeless musicians who play through the night. Melancholy pervades, a sense of time fleeting, a rose before the petals fall. Outside, the cafes, shops, and drinking houses blink on their lights. And since it is a damp Christmas Eve, an Irish coffee, cognac, or Miller on tap warms the sight. The French Quarter has always attracted the rich and poor to close the door on guilt and savor life.

ACT ONE

SCENE 1

(The present. The apartment is piled with medical books and a bare Christmas tree. BLAINE and GILLIAN are kissing heavily. Bells from the Saint Louis Cathedral chime, a jazz version of "Jingle Bells" clangs from the street, and the doorbell rings nonstop. Offstage SARA pounds the building door and screams out to DALE, who is unloading SARA's Cadillac, then through the intercom at BLAINE. BLAINE talks into the intercom with one voice and to GILLIAN with another.)

BLAINE. Battered by bells.

SARA. *(Offstage. Into intercom.)* I'm downstairs. Loaded with boxes. Your father's things.

BLAINE. My aunt.

SARA. *(Offstage. To DALE)* Dale!

BLAINE. Ugh! We'll have to make love later.

(A crash. BLAINE jumps.)

GILLIAN. *(Breathing heavily, to BLAINE)* Don't stop. I'm on fire—

BLAINE. I don't want her to meet you like this.

GILLIAN. The only thing that's not hot is my feet.

(SOUND: Banging and yelling outside.)

(BLAINE pulls on his shirt.)

SARA. *(Offstage. Into intercom.)* Blaine?

GILLIAN. *(To BLAINE)* Don't answer. I know it seems like an extravagance—

BLAINE. Is the door locked?

GILLIAN. Your prioritizing romance—

SARA. *(Offstage. Into intercom.)* Help me bring this junk up.

BLAINE. *(Into intercom)* Merry Christmas, Aunt Sara.

GILLIAN. *(Erotically to* **BLAINE***)* Say you're busy.

BLAINE. *(Relenting. Into intercom)* You're two hours early.

SARA. *(Offstage)* The Christmas party is always at six o'clock.

BLAINE. *(Into intercom)* Could you please get some ice?

SARA. *(Offstage. Into intercom)* I've got your father's suits.

GILLIAN. I've something to show you.

BLAINE. Stop!

SARA. *(Offstage)* I donated them to the Junior League—After his funeral. But your sister bought them back.

BLAINE. *(Into intercom)* I'm buzzing you in; don't leave those clothes.

GILLIAN. It's not my fault you're so damn gorgeous—and I can't take my hands off you.

BLAINE. *(Breathing heavily)* Button up your blouse!

GILLIAN. Do I need to start—the good old Southern tradition...of begging for it—

BLAINE. The third button.

GILLIAN. Begin our own Gothic history.

BLAINE. If you're going to punish me, I'm going downstairs.

(Offstage. Feet pounding upstairs.)

BLAINE. *(To* **GILLIAN***)* Aunt Sara's arrival is one of a series of catastrophes. I talked to her four hours yesterday. I set myself up to be tortured. Used to be there wasn't much to do but listen. I've perfected two phrases with her: "Em," and "There you have it."

SARA. *(Offstage)* How many flights are in this rat trap? Two?

BLAINE. There you have it. *(To* **GILLIAN***)* Help me clean up.

GILLIAN. *(Flops back on chaise)* I'm too excited.

BLAINE. My aunt's a relic from another stratosphere. She's like...black ice. You can't see it, but it's treacherous. *(Looks around)* Where are my shoes?

SARA. *(Offstage)* I've made it to the first floor.

BLAINE. *(To* **GILLIAN***)* She's coming in. End of sentence.

GILLIAN. You didn't tell her we're getting married.

BLAINE. I didn't want to...expose you to my family. Until I was sure...Sweetness and elegance in a relationship are such beautiful things.

GILLIAN. If she's not nice, is the marriage off?

BLAINE. No. The marriage is on with alien relatives. I know this sounds neurotic. *(He swallows dryly.)* But could you...go out into the courtyard...and come back in...*(Swallows again)* so I can present you.

GILLIAN. I don't believe this—

BLAINE. *(To* **GILLIAN***. Clearing his throat excessively)* You have to understand that if you're family connected, there's a certain liability.

GILLIAN. Where in the hell's my purse?

BLAINE. Watch the expletives.

GILLIAN. Where's my fucking purse? *(Breathing quickly)* By thirty, I feel, it's time for me.

SARA. *(Offstage. Using a key)* Open up!

BLAINE. *(Whispers to* **GILLIAN***)* God, she's got a key.

GILLIAN. You gave her a—

BLAINE. No...Quick, into the bedroom.

*(***GILLIAN*** ducks into the bedroom.* **SARA** *staggers into the room, out of breath and feigning chest pains. She is wearing a long glamorous velvet gown, a hat, and a fur and is dragging a bag of suits.)*

BLAINE. Merry Christmas. You're sure enough early.

SARA. *(Gasping)* I'm going to have my lawyers...contact your landlord...because I didn't have a heart condition...till I climbed those stairs.

BLAINE. *(Steering her)* How did you get the key?

SARA. Don't fuss at me.

BLAINE. Aunt Sara, you can't just barge in here.

SARA. *(Collapses in a chair, panting)* If I see one more tee-shirt with a Cajun Christmas tree, I'll vomit. *(Looks about)* Shall I set these suits in your bedroom?

BLAINE. I'll take them.

*(***DALE*** enters in a long velvet coat. She lugs ornaments, a huge nativity set, and a man's Xmas sweater. She gasps for breath.)*

DALE. Oh, Blaine, let me hug you. I saved you Dad's sweater.

BLAINE. Wait. I don't want this stuff—

SARA. You haven't taken the time to lie and say I look pretty. My husband, God rest his soul, lied to me for three years, and I was in bliss.

BLAINE. You look beautiful. There you have it.

SARA. Dale, go put my hat and coat on the bed.

BLAINE. I'll take it.

(Grabs the coat and hat and hurries them to the bedroom.)

SARA. Let me look at you, Blaine.

DALE. He's not finished dressing?

SARA. I've the one good eye. I see well, but I don't see details. You don't look like yourself.
BLAINE. I haven't combed my hair.

SARA. Your buttons are mismatched. There is a great difference between being casual and being sloppy. Your character is in your shirt. You've lost weight. Why won't you come to dinner?

DALE. *(Touching him)* You used to come every Friday and Sunday. Aunt Sara would have such spreads, crabmeat au gratin, baby asparagus, and crawfish bisque. Let me fix your hair.

SARA. If you're sick of seafood, Bertha could make grilled quail or lacquered duck.

DALE. Why not come once a week?

BLAINE. I plan to. I phone y'all—

DALE. Tell us what you want and when you're coming now, and we'll start planning ahead—

BLAINE. I can't, sugar. I'm sorry. It's hard when people move away. I know. You feel like it's part of yourself you're losing. But I'll be back. Soon as I graduate, I'll visit a lot.

DALE. Let me sit by you. Now you tell me your schedule, and I'll help you find a time—

BLAINE. *(Clenches his teeth)* Not now!

DALE. Give me your hand.

BLAINE. God, I'm loaded with my studies. I don't get off class till four—I've no time.

DALE. I don't want you to stay away.

BLAINE. Things are better now. I still miss y'all, but I'm living a saner life. I no longer drink a bottle of Maalox a day.

SARA. You're not studying too hard? Knowledge counts, but it doesn't count that much in building a practice. Medicine's still a social art. Whenever I call my plastic surgeon, which I do regularly, he's off skiing in Lake Tahoe. *(Points to a paper wallet)* Your tuition, rent, and lagniappe.

BLAINE. Thanks.

SARA. Course I've no idea how long I'll be able to help you. I've never balanced a checkbook. I shrivel at the thought. Shrivel!

BLAINE. After med school, I'll spoil you...

DALE. I kept Dad's medical kit for you. With the initials outside. Mm. The leather's still fresh. Won't you wear Dad's Christmas sweater?

SARA. Stop emoting, Dale.

DALE. A pine needle's still in the sleeve. Here, I'll help you.

BLAINE. No. *(His voice breaks)* I don't want to be like Dad.

SARA. It's horrible, but I can't show any interest in death.

BLAINE. *(Rushes to the door)* All right, that's it. I don't want these suits, this case, this sweater. I don't want to head the Am. Med. Assoc., treat all the indigents in Louisiana, bury my wife at thirty-five, and die myself at fifty-three. Take this stuff back.

(SOUND: The Cathedral bells toll.)

(DALE rushes out, suddenly triggered, crazed.)

DALE. Oh, no. Blaine's a monster. He hates dead people. Oh no...I must get to Church.

BLAINE. *(Yells out)* Dale. Come back. Dale.

SARA. She's off to the Cathedral. *(She undoes her collar. Gasps)* Your sister is a mortuary fanatic. I don't know why I took her in. You ever hear of a funeral cortege on Christmas Eve? She's given me a fever.

BLAINE. You let her run around by herself in the Quarter?

SARA. Joe will follow her.

BLAINE. Who?

SARA. My new escort. He's changed his name from Joel.

BLAINE. Shouldn't you go too—

SARA. Don't punish me, Blaine, I can't go with her. I'm too embarrassed. *(Throws herself back in the chair, panting)* Dale makes us stop by each funeral service so she can pay her respects. She wants people passing by her funeral—to drop in.

BLAINE. *(Hands her some water)* Drink this. You're dehydrated. It's not easy to understand Dale because she's so much going on inside. Her hormones are raging, and her heart is bigger—

SARA. When I said I'd take her, I thought it'd be mostly weekends. There is some weirdness in her, and I can't figure it out. She got kicked out of boarding school because they thought she was a witch. They found her in City Park feeding chicken to the alligators. Grape and magnolia leaves all through her hair.

BLAINE. You never told me.

SARA. Mud all over the car upholstery and—*(Gulps. Removes a sack of items from her purse)* Yesterday I found these strange articles of personal adornment inside her clothes: animal claws, tiny carved owls. Look in the bag. It's too dreadful.

BLAINE. They called Joan of Ark a witch, and—What's this?

SARA. A bird head. Dale's possessed. She howls at night like an inhuman soul. When half of your family is gone, you're a psychological amputee. Check my heart. The girl terrifies me.

BLAINE. *(Awkwardly reaches his stethoscope down her shirt)* If you can keep Dale busy enough, she won't notice—

SARA. You're gone? I hate to be the bad fairy, but you've got to come live with us. When you pass on an errand, Dale starts watching for your MG.

BLAINE. If she's unhappy without me, she'll be unhappy with me. Med school's intense; it's bound to strain my relationships. *(Puts away stethoscope)* You're fine, Aunt Sara.

SARA. But for how long?

BLAINE. I'll get the *hors d'oeuvres*.

(SOUND: Knee-tapping guitarist plays "Oh Holy Night, the Stars are Brightly Shining. T'is the Night, of the Dear Savior's Birth.")

(SARA hurries to the balcony.)

SARA. The Quarter is swarming with junkies. Awful signs, "I'll work for food." I suppose I should throw them some quarters.

(BLAINE sneaks GILLIAN from the bedroom out the front door.)

SARA. Hey Joe! That adorable man. Dumb as a post. He just drives me about. Last week, Joe dropped Dale off and didn't find her till six hours later. There's not a square block in the Quarter. It's built around bayous, rivers, and coolies. *(Sniffs and picks up a long hair strand.)* Funny smell, like lavender perfume. *(Finds a purse and snoops inside)* Whose purse? Tampax. What's this? A birth control device?

BLAINE. *(Coming out to the balcony with a tray of goodies)* Don't start.

SARA. Where did "Don't Start" go? Remember, Blaine. What one needs in the dark of the night, one tosses out in the morning. I hope you're going to Mass and confession. *(Chuckles)*

BLAINE. Chocolates?

SARA. Never eat chocolate. Rots the teeth.

BLAINE. Cashews?

SARA. I'm watching my waist now that I can see it. You have any shrimp puffs or crab dip? I didn't come here to eat from plastic. *(BLAINE passes her a dish.)* Canned cheese straws? So, who is she?

BLAINE. My life has swerved in a new direction. It's the most extraordinary thing. I met this actress—

SARA. All your breeding, and you can't get a proper date and decent canapes. I hire help in threes. Three maids, three cooks, three drivers. One always shows up, and you can fire two when necessary.

BLAINE. *(Controlling his temper)* It's hard for you to understand, you've been so grief-struck about Dad.

SARA. Grief-struck? I never saw your father. Still, it is a plunge in appearances.

BLAINE. For all the woman I've dated, Gillian's the most magical with her long hair and—

SARA. Mm. Your cheese straws are limp.

BLAINE. I'm engaged.

SARA. There's no reason not to be dreaming about marriage, but to commit to it. You spend your thirties doing that. Don't spend your twenties doing it.

BLAINE. Gillian's not like other women. She's traveled to Australia, lived in Africa. She lives her life completely from her conscience.

SARA. Hmph. Is she well connected? To have an image in the medical community, you must have a wife who appears first-rate as wives go. You've a family tree going back to…to—

BLAINE. Jesus Christ.

SARA. Who are her parents?

BLAINE. Her father was a mortician.

SARA. A mortician's daughter? And an actress. You wouldn't be accepted in any social home in the South. I can hear your table conversation. "What's the latest in shrouds?"

BLAINE. Are you relaxed?

SARA. No.

BLAINE. I'm getting married on January sixth.

SARA. In a year.

BLAINE. In two weeks. On the Epiphany. The day the angels changed the wise men's lives. I was pretty much hopeless, you see. If it wasn't for prayer, I'd have been suicidal. I met Gillian...she's so balanced. She's always—
there. Even when she's away, she's always there. The problem with many marriages is there's no magic. Good woman, nice family, very competent. Those women cannot help you move out of your deficits.

SARA. That's ridiculous.

BLAINE. I'm looking for a new form, breaking the envelope.

SARA. If I'd known you had to settle down, I would have fixed you up with the LaBorde girl.

BLAINE. *(Giggles)* We've no chemistry.

SARA. How about English? Physics? At least you know you don't like each other. What's so funny?

BLAINE. The reason I've this giddy feeling is I keep thinking I'm not qualified for a wife like Gillian, and someday, somebody is going to call me on this. I'm waiting any minute for some shoe to drop or midnight to arrive.

SARA. You're afraid she'll be exposed as a fraud.

BLAINE. Oh, Aunt Sara. There's nothing more wonderful than to marry the woman you care about the most. Having a sweetheart, something inside of you lightens and you're not out there by yourself anymore. I thought I'd take a leave from school, bask in the happiness, but Gillian wants to get married over the break, and there's an opening at the Cathedral.

SARA. Why don't you just kill me? Hang my clothes next to your father's. Lay me out at the mortuary.

BLAINE. Please. I'm not an eel. I don't have tough skin.

SARA. How's Dale going to take this wedding? A girl who isn't even smart enough to hang around with the outcasts? Oh, some days she's normal, but I never know when those days are.

BLAINE. The family is important to me so we'll get together. Gillian's helped me thread my life together. She has more energy than other people. The energy of a singular person.

SARA. All of her family are dead?

BLAINE. Yes.

SARA. She has no relatives? No contacts? The system for success is contacts. *(A Cadillac horn screeches.* **SARA** *waves and yells.)* Hey, Dale. Dale. She wears James' gold cross as if she's taken on your father as a cult.

BLAINE. No one accepts death at once. We get eased into it. Dale was okay before. She'll revert back. Remember when I took her to London. We went walking on the heath, and she started to accept Dad's illness—

SARA. Dale gets depressed. Six hours a day I can't find her. I thought minding her would get easier. It didn't. The episodes got greater. But you're distracted, and my chest pains mean nothing.

BLAINE. You have nervous indigestion from getting too excited, worked up all the time. The meat. The booze. If you'd start an exercise program—

SARA. I'm turning into an old woman fast, teeth falling out, wrinkles crawling over the skin.

BLAINE. *(Giggles)* I want you to help me organize the wedding.

SARA. You don't have a knife or a gun?

BLAINE. I'm getting married!

SARA. You're gaga.

BLAINE. I'm going to have a wife!

SARA. Nuts.

BLAINE. I didn't want to get married now. But being with Gillian is like walking on the moon. Once you've done that the world has a different perspective.

SARA. The most awful thing that's happened in marriage is aunts having abdicated their traditional function as marriage-makers.

*(**DALE** enters, breathing heavily. She catches her breath in the doorway.)*

DALE. Who's getting...married, Blaine?

SARA. Your brother's discussing a couple he used to know.

DALE. In the...French Quarter?

SARA. No. Most households in the Quarter are selfish people, living alone.

BLAINE. Bing.

SARA. *(Shouts to **DALE**)* Come in. Entrance ways are for people who don't know one another.

*(**DALE** removes her coat. She is wearing a nun's habit and is short of breath.)*

DALE. Oh, Blaine. You missed the best funeral. Five Cardinals in the same church. Of course, one was dead. Lucky me, I arrived in time for them to make their exit. One came from Africa. One was on crutches. One was being helped by two people—

BLAINE. What's that get-up? *(Takes her coat to the bedroom)*

DALE. It's a ceremonial habit. I've joined a religious order—the Lazarians.

BLAINE. The what?

SARA. Some lay cult obsessed with the dead. Thank God she goes out at dawn and dusk, the antisocial hours.

DALE. Let's set out the Christmas ornaments. *(Walks to the side)* I'll put up the manger. Dad used to read Saint Luke: *(Gasps)* "Mary gave birth to her first-born son and wrapped him in swaddling clothes and...laid him in a manger, because—"

SARA. "There was no room for them in the inn."

BLAINE. *(To SARA)* Her shortness of breath seems worse. I'm looking at my sister a moment ago. I've no idea what's going on in her life. A lay cult?

SARA. It's a catastrophe. I told her. If you enter the cloister, you'll have killed your aunt. I won't visit you. Stick my face behind an iron grill. *(To BLAINE)* I demand you come live with us.

DALE. Can I sit on your lap? *(Sits on his lap, unwraps statues)* Here's Balthasar, your favorite wise man. And his camel.

BLAINE. The ox, with a crack down his back.

DALE. And the donkey with one ear—

SARA. We can put baby Jesus in the cradle before his time has come. *(To BLAINE)* Tell Dale about your plans.

BLAINE. *(To DALE)* I've met a wonderful woman. She's kind and gentle—

DALE. Don't talk about her. Talk about me. Look, I've got the star from our old manger set. *(Hugs him)*

SARA. Your brother's going...to ruin his life with a certain—

(GILLIAN enters, lingering in the doorway in a superb evening dress.)

GILLIAN. Gillian Pederson-Krag. Merry Christmas.

SARA. *(To* **GILLIAN***)* Stand up, Dale.

BLAINE. Honey, this is my aunt, Sara Birdsong. The pretty girl's my sister, Dale. This is Gillian, my fiancée.

SARA. Peculiar name—Pederson-Krag. Is that one or two words?

GILLIAN. I was married before.

SARA. What did "our" husband do?

GILLIAN. Not enough.

BLAINE. You don't have to apologize for having been married.

GILLIAN. I'm not. *(To* **SARA***)* What a lovely pin.

SARA. I don't like snakes, but they're the symbol of medicine, and my family is in that business.

DALE. *(To* **GILLIAN***)* They're also the symbol of fertility. Did you know that?

GILLIAN. I'm not pregnant.

BLAINE. *(Breaking free of* **DALE***)* Dale. Finish fixing the stable.

SARA. The Dominican nuns gave your father that manger set. James treated the entire order and never charged a cent.

DALE. *(To* **GILLIAN***)* There's my father's picture.

GILLIAN. Nice.

DALE. Look if you move back and forth, his eyes follow you around. Wonderful eyes.

SARA. With those tarantula lashes.

DALE. Just like Blaine's. Come sit by me, Blaine.

BLAINE. Not now, honey.

DALE. Oh, Blaine's so cold.

SARA. In my day, women were supposed to entertain. You talked about dogs or the weather.

*(The following lines overlap as **DALE** interrupts to get attention.)*

BLAINE. *(To **GILLIAN**)* Tell my family about your acting career.

GILLIAN. I got cast on this medical show—

DALE. My father was a grand loving doctor.

GILLIAN. I see. It's a hospital series for—

DALE. One call, one chat, one round of visits.

GILLIAN. Actually, I play this head nurse—

DALE. My father liked tradition. He guarded his patients.

SARA. Gillian doesn't want to talk about your father. The middle classes don't have an obsession with parenting.

BLAINE. What was that crack for?

SARA. It was a joke.

BLAINE. Don't joke about Gillian. Joke about—*(Searches for a name)* Joe.

SARA. My niece and nephew are the image of their father. Altruistic and obsessive—Of course I like being single. Most women do. Women have got to marry men older or uglier or poorer 'cause the world prefers men. And women have got to be smarter because men say they'll take care of us, but they don't. And now when you look around—there's a crop failure in men. So I suppose I'll never have another. Still, I was married happily for three years, three years out of ten, that's pretty good. *(Smiles)* Hand me the chocolates, Dale.

GILLIAN. We'd like to have the reception in your home.

SARA. Who's organizing this?

BLAINE. Of course we could elope, but in a way it leaves us bereft. We're nostalgic for the rituals that make life important.
DALE. I got something caught in my throat.

SARA. She eats too fast.

BLAINE. Swallow, sugar.

DALE. I can't breathe.

SARA. And then her windpipe is too small.

GILLIAN. Hurry.

DALE. Something is stuck.

BLAINE. I'll get it. The Heimlich.

DALE. *(Coughs up the chocolate)* There it is. Oh no. I'm so embarrassed.

BLAINE. Ssh. Go rest...Lie down here. Relax.

GILLIAN. Dale, I brought you a gift. A friendship ring. See, the tiny bands come entwined like wreaths.

BLAINE. Say, "thank you," sugar.

DALE. I hate jewelry.

BLAINE. That's not nice. Symmetry Jewelers even engraved it.

DALE. My father died, and left me a sapphire with forty diamonds. I would rather have had him alive. I never wear it.

GILLIAN. Not this ring?

DALE. Blaine gave you my sapphire. It belonged to my grandmother.

SARA. That ring's been around.

DALE. She stole my ring. Daddy gave it to me. No. No. No— *(She covers her ears and runs to the balcony.)*

BLAINE. It was in Dad's bank box in a blue velvet bag with my initials on it.

GILLIAN. I didn't take your ring. Excuse me, I feel...nauseous. *(Exits away from* **DALE** *to the bedroom.)*

BLAINE. Dad told me to use it, if I ever needed an engagement ring before—

SARA. How old is that woman?

BLAINE. Gillian—you okay?

GILLIAN. *(Calling back)* I'm a young twenty-nine...

BLAINE. You've gotten Gillian upset.

SARA. Oh, she came in upset. Live in the real world.

BLAINE. What is the real world? It's got something to do with feelings. I'm telling you, this is the most thrilling time of my life...And you're not listening. I can't be near you because of the— I want you to like Gillian.

SARA. And what about my hurt? Usually I repress my feelings, but tonight I can't.

BLAINE. Em.

SARA. My first Christmas with Dale, and you pay no attention to me.

BLAINE. You don't get a lot of attention because people are anxious around you. It's like people recognize it when they see it, but they don't know what it is— rudeness.

SARA. How dare you?

(SOUND: The Cathedral bells toll.)

DALE. *(Rushes in from the balcony)* My father was a grand loving doctor. One call, one chat, one round of visits. *(Stomps feet and removes a stuffed duck from her purse)* One call, one chat, one round of visits.

SARA. Some days Dale'll be nice, and others she throws this at you. She's doing this more this week than ever before. You have to get used to it. *(Pulls the duck out of Dale's hand)* She sleeps with that little beat-up terrycloth duck you gave her when she was five. Carries it everywhere. *(Whispers)* Have you forgotten the boarding school? She was crying so much, she stopped eating. And all those tiresome stories about Dale trying to wound herself. The last time it was at breakfast with a grapefruit knife. *(Shaking her head)* Roll up your sleeves, Dale.

DALE. No.

SARA. *(Tears back her sleeves)* There.

BLAINE. You cut your wrists.

DALE. No. I was goofing off. The knife slipped.

BLAINE. Don't lie.

DALE. Stop screaming. They're just scratches.

SARA. She does it to torment me! This morning I was so upset, I cut my lip, and it swelled up so bad, I couldn't wear lipstick. I've got to use the little girls' room.

(SARA exits to the bathroom.)

DALE. Come live with us.

BLAINE. I can't. Saturday, I'll visit, and we'll talk.

DALE. No, you won't.

BLAINE. Going to med school is really hard.

DALE. I wouldn't bother you.

BLAINE. All that reading makes your brain tight. I've this pretty nice arrangement where I can go to class from eight to four, rest for an hour or so, then study all night.

DALE. You could have the whole attic.

BLAINE. What makes it possible to face up to so much work is the relaxation I get from coming home alone. That soothing interlude before study. The calm before the letting go of the day. I love it when television's off, and the phone doesn't ring. You have to be fairly independent to be a good medical student.

DALE. Then why are you getting married?

BLAINE. When you're in love, you don't have this gnawing feeling in your gut. You're fed by this wonderful ambiance. You study harder, longer. *(Looks up and sees* **GILLIAN***)* Gillian.

GILLIAN. *(Returning from the bedroom)* I freshened up, and I feel better. *(To* **DALE***)* I'm sorry I took your ring. Here.

DALE. I don't want it.

GILLIAN. Won't you forgive me...be in our wedding? I ordered you a beautiful dress.

BLAINE. And a rose bouquet. You can have all the Shirley Temples and *petit fours* you want.

DALE. *(Backs onto the balcony with* **BLAINE** *and* **GILLIAN** *following)* I don't want things! They're carrying that dead Cardinal to the hearse now. See the stream of cars. The headlights. The trumpets at the door.

BLAINE. My loving Gillian has nothing to do with my love for you. I love her in a different way, but I've loved you longer. You can spend every Saturday night with us, and after med school, we'll see about a room for you.

DALE. No, you won't. You'll forget.

GILLIAN. Soon, you'll go off to college.

*(***SARA** *crosses into the bedroom for her hat and coat.)*

DALE. Not for two years. Living with Aunt Sara is horrible. The woman should collapse under the weight of her own awfulness. When she comes to my room, it's like the arrival of Valkyries.

BLAINE. I know she can be a pain, sugar, but—

SARA. *(Crossing to the balcony with her hat and the two coats)* Oh, do be nice to Dale after she's been so ugly. This has been the most dreadful Christmas. Blaine screaming at me and making me depressed. It's awful to have ugly things said about you. It's even worse to have them said in front of strangers unexpectedly.

DALE. I wanted to explain to Blaine—

SARA. *(Hands* **DALE** *her coat)* Put on your coat. I took you in so Blaine could triumph in med school, not so he could marry an overaged woman. You and Gillian are colluding against me.

GILLIAN. That's not true.

SARA. It's something when wives turn out to be nobodies. Mediocrity and availability will beat out background and intelligence any day. *(To* **BLAINE***)* If you insist on marrying that woman, I'll keep Dale for one week after the honeymoon, then she can move in with you.

BLAINE. Dale can't live here.

SARA. It's emotionally debilitating. You're a thief. You've stolen my youth.

DALE. I'm moving in with Gillian and Blaine. Wow!

SARA. *(Waves)* Joe, we're coming!

DALE. Gee! I can't wait to live here! This is the most exciting news—

SARA. Stop raving! The French Quarter is so ugly. It's Gentilly times fifty.

*(***SARA*** leaves with* **DALE*.)**

SCENE 2

(Continuous)

GILLIAN. *(Searches for a Kleenex in her purse)* Where's my purse?

BLAINE. *(Points)* I'm sorry. I should have warned you—

GILLIAN. I'm dumbfounded.

BLAINE. In this family, you need two personalities. The private one and the one that gets beaten on. If only I wasn't in touch with the one that's beaten on. *(Chuckles)*

GILLIAN. *(Sniffs)* Stop.

BLAINE. I'll get us some coffee. After Dad's death, I vowed I'd live in the real world, try to be generous and caring, but I tell you it's frightening. To some extent, I can comfort myself with the thought we've been down difficult paths before.

GILLIAN. Don't say anything.

BLAINE. I want to help...make the hurt go away.

GILLIAN. Leave me be.

BLAINE. *(Romantically)* My perspective is very multifaceted as a result of this lifetime in medicine. I started when I was sixteen years old by lying about my age and getting a job at Touro Hospital—

GILLIAN. Stop.

BLAINE. Because I was passionate about healing and wanted to be near doctors and at that point thought they were just a step below the gods. Of course you learn otherwise when you move around with them in the world.

GILLIAN. Don't touch me.

BLAINE. Right. Coffee? Cream? Sugar?

GILLIAN. Bourbon, if available.

BLAINE. Whoa!
GILLIAN. Take Dale this ring. How could you give it to me when—

BLAINE. She said she hated jewelry.

GILLIAN. I can't live with you and your sister. I'm not the same as the girls you've dated. Something's missing on my face. I look up and I can't find it. I think it's youth.

BLAINE. You're young.

GILLIAN. I'm thirty-four. I lied to your aunt. *(Nervously)* All of my problems are related to my body. I've a seriously screwed-up body. And then, there's the whole question of kids.

BLAINE. You don't want children, fine.

GILLIAN. Something you can't have is rather difficult to want. Children aren't yours, they're on loan anyway. Three years ago I was in an accident. I probably can't have kids. No portraits to ornament the parlor. No sons to champion your name.

BLAINE. *(Swallows hard)* Children count in marriage, but they don't count that much.

GILLIAN. I'm thirty-five.

BLAINE. You want to stop with that number now? Or shall we go on?

GILLIAN. I'm thirty-six. When you said Dale was sixteen, I envisioned this child. She's complicated and so is my career. How can an actress's life be compatible with a strong man's?

BLAINE. No point in being afraid of a strong man, you should be afraid of a crazy man. I can't live with romantic ambivalence.

GILLIAN. I am not nineteen and naive anymore. There aren't many auditions in New Orleans, and when my agent calls, I have to be ready to travel. I can't tell you when I'm coming home, if I'm on tour— What if I get a Broadway play that's held over?

BLAINE. I'll grab my suitcases, borrow money from the bank, and take a plane to New York.

GILLIAN. It's not a relationship when you're living with someone who's not there. My work is my obsession. When you're an actress, you help create soul in the universe. The theater calls for energy, a mythic closeness. You are stripping yourself, exposing your life, in all your failings, so you can provide insight to others. Acting is religious. It 's my mission. What an actress passes on is finally her soul.

BLAINE. That's wonderful. I'll save the bodies and you save the souls...Most of my friends think I'm nuts going to med school when I've got to follow him. *(Points to his father's portrait)* My dad gave his life to surgery. And he was incredible. He could tell what was wrong with a person by the way he walked. And sometimes he actually cured people by laying on his hands and saying you'll be okay. People lined up in front of his clinic for blocks...just to see him. Maybe it was because he didn't charge them. Something that made my mother slam doors and scream at him in their bedroom. If people couldn't pay their bill, he would rip it up. And at Christmas time deliveries of food, flowers, and plants would begin: overwhelming the house with the aroma of joy and gratitude. When he died, Dad had two thousand dollars in his account. He said, "Well, that's two thousand dollars more than I had when I came in." Aunt Sara bailed us out. Unless I get through med school, there won't be much future for me or Dale.

GILLIAN. Oh, Blaine.

BLAINE. What I miss most about him is his idealism, this sense of mission, which you have. Tell me we're better than any other couple.

GILLIAN. Yes. We're both so...damn needy.

BLAINE. You are beautiful. *(BLAINE whistles)*

GILLIAN. Don't whistle.

BLAINE. You used to like it.

GILLIAN. I like everything about you. That's the problem.

BLAINE. Marry me. *(Hugging her)* It never feels like you're strong, when you're doing something important, it feels like you're on the abyss. *(They kiss.)*

SCENE 3

(Ten a.m., twelve days later, January 6th. Sun blasts through the windows, giving the apartment a stark reality. **SARA** *enters in a long black dress, a veil over her face. She is crying. She sits in a corner sniveling into her champagne.* **DALE,** *who looks much paler, wears an airy pink bridesmaid's dress. She puts out some strawberries. Offstage,* **GILLIAN** *is in the kitchen in her wedding dress, and* **BLAINE,** *in his morning suit, is downstairs in front of the apartment.)*

DALE. Pink is for dancing. *(Spins about, eating)* The Cathedral was lovely. Incense and organ music. The private wedding—

BLAINE. *(Offstage)* All the bags packed?

GILLIAN. *(Offstage)* Not yet.

DALE. I can't wait for the reception.

SARA. *(Sobbing)* Now Blaine's married. I feel so old—You'll be moving.

BLAINE. *(Offstage)*You got the Euros?

GILLIAN. Yep.

SARA. *(Sobs to* **DALE***)* What shall I do? Take a correspondence course in antiques? Volunteer at the hospital? Have a face lift? When you're young, you're too hot to handle, and when you're ready, no one wants to handle you.

GILLIAN. *(Peeks in)* Check the passports on the mantle.

DALE. *(Checks the mantle)* They're okay!

SARA. Have you seen my neighbor? Angelina looks like a younger version of herself, like she's left town and her cousin's arrived. Angelina says to me, "How old are you? Fifty?" Let's get to the point. She was on the operating table twelve hours, with three plastic surgeons.

DALE. When Daddy was a boy, at Jesuit High School, the priests made them say "Congratulations" at weddings. *(Picking at the strawberries)* When Daddy was alive we ate lots of strawberries. I thought the stork dropped me from a planet where they made them. Daddy fed me—

SARA. If you say Daddy once more—I'll scream.

BLAINE. *(Entering)* Where are the plane tickets?

SARA. You want them now?

BLAINE. I'm going to stick them in my carry-on.

*(She hands them to **BLAINE**, who starts reading them over. **GILLIAN** enters.)*

SARA. Open them later. It's a midnight flight. And the hotel accommodations are paid for. We should be going.

GILLIAN. Thanks again, Aunt Sara.

SARA. Sara.

GILLIAN. I've always wanted to go to Paris. Then to stay in the wedding suite at the *George V* near the *Champs Elysées* with a grand piano and a balcony view of the Eiffel Tower.

(SOUND: Car toots.)

SARA. We've got to get to the Country Club.

GILLIAN. I dread facing your relatives again. Tough crowd. If they only pretended to care about me, I could take it. You know I once had a nosebleed during an audition, but I wanted the part so bad I stuffed a Kleenex in my nose and continued acting. The director kept yelling. Finally, I screamed, "I'm bleeding. What do you want?" "Another actress," he said.

BLAINE. You look gorgeous...You have this emotional translucence. Everyone loved your hair with the pearl insets.

GILLIAN. Why did your cousins stare at me?

SARA. Let's go down...

GILLIAN. Is it because of my age? One woman said I looked like your mother.

BLAINE. I'm sure it was meant as a compliment. My mother was beautiful, and died young.

SARA. *(Checks her watch)* Get my fur, Dale. My eyes are all puffy. My face looks like a tomato. My hat's on the bed.

DALE. We're not going down before Gillian. *(Pushes her down)* I'll sit in your lap if I have to.

SARA. *(Forces her off)* Get off. You monster. Let me go.

BLAINE. These tickets say January first. There must be some mistake.

SARA. It must be a seven.

BLAINE. And our hotel reservations are for last week.

GILLIAN. What's going on?

BLAINE. I don't know. Aunt Sara?

SARA. I feel so wretched...It was the maid's fault. She was supposed to check them. But she's—illiterate. A liar. The new maid, Luella, Suella, I can't pronounce it. Why is everyone glaring at me? You don't suspect I did this? *(Gasps)* Joe picked up the tickets.

DALE. If you hadn't been juiced up sobbing all week—Oh...You're so mean.

SARA. Who do you think paid the caterer—

GILLIAN. Oh...no.

SARA. Ordered the roses—

BLAINE. Don't cry. Please. We'll call. We'll fix this after the reception.

SARA. Made a donation to the Cathedral. Glamour doesn't come cheap.

DALE. You ruined their trip.

SARA. Then to be attacked by a brooding sixteen-year-old...and a woman I never liked in the first place.

DALE. You're a cruel, lousy witch! *(Starts to exit)*

SARA. Fine, Dale. You go to the reception alone. Spend the night with Blaine. I was going to keep you till after the honeymoon, but you've been so vicious, you can stay with them. My niece is a heart thief on a monumental scale. She's chewed up my feelings and spit them out.

(SARA exits. DALE calls after her.)

DALE. What a thrill to move in early. Have Joe bring my stuff.

BLAINE. *(Calls after her)* Aunt Sara.

DALE. My terrycloth duck? My pictures?

(Cadillac roars off)

GILLIAN. She's left. This morning, I got dressed, put on this veil, your aunt says to me, "I suspect Dale will move in sooner than you think."

BLAINE. Let me hold you.

DALE. Where are we going tonight?

BLAINE. We could check in a hotel.

GILLIAN. With her?

DALE. I'll keep quiet and hidden like a good little mouse.

GILLIAN. *(Whispers)* You can't have sex when you don't have hope.

BLAINE. Shh. We've got to get to the reception.

GILLIAN. *(Yells)* You go. I agreed to take Dale in temporarily. Not give up my life.

(DALE *circles about them, flitting about them, like a butterfly, placing objects here and there as the light fades.*)

SCENE FOUR

(Two months later. Early March, Mardi Gras time. The living room is strewn with **DALE***'s objects and Mardi Gras decorations and costumes.* **SARA** *in a long coat is talking into a cell phone. She walks before the set as if down a street.)*

SARA. Blaine. Are you there? Pick up…No, I don't want to leave a message so you can wave my laundry over the Quarter. I'll call back. *(Hangs up and dials again)* This is your aunt. Remember? The one who is financing your education. I don't like the role, but I've got to play it. Pick up. *(Slams the phone and dials again)* Blaine, I know you're there. Medical school's over, and it's five-thirty. I got your exam grades. Need I say, I'm horrified. I don't want to be hectored by F reports showing up in my mailbox. When I said medicine was a social art, I didn't mean it was a party. You have my brother's reputation to consider. *(Coughs)* I know the roots of stupidity are complex, but I want you to get your brain out of hock. Learning is a slow system of osmosis. Eavesdrop on the smart fellows. Write a longer paper. And please do brown-nose your teachers after class. *(Coughs)* Remember the golden rule. She who has the gold rules. I'm not financing a failure.

(Blackout. Toward the end of **SARA***'s speech,* **DALE** *enters in a sorcerer's costume with her astrology chart.* **GILLIAN** *follows, retreating to a corner to rehearse her nurse's role in the television series.* **BLAINE** *crosses to another part of the room, studying. Throughout the scene, street revelers scream out, "Throw me some beads," or play music, something like, "All because it's carnival time, it's carnival ti-me, it's carnival ti-me, everybody's drinking wine," as they await the approach of a parade.)*

DALE. Blaine has the most wonderful astrology chart. There's so much creative giftedness around him, I've been inhaling.

GILLIAN. Shh. I'm working on my lines.

DALE. Still?

GILLIAN. You have to make art as if you had eternity. *(Studies her script)* "The doctor will be making rounds in a half an hour if you'd like to freshen up."

BLAINE. *(Puts headsets to his ears and opens a book)* I'm going under. Do you know the Australian box jellyfish is the most poisonous one alive? Toxins, that's the theme of the night.

DALE. *(To BLAINE)* Look. I did a watercolor of your sun sign, maybe finished, maybe not. Blaine's an old soul. He's had twenty-five hundred lives.

GILLIAN. Get that out of his face.

DALE. I just goof off...nearly every day. Mama studied at the *École des Beaux Arts*, and lived on Beethoven Street—in Paris.

GILLIAN. "What are these pills doing here? You were supposed to take them—"

DALE. Across from the Eiffel Tower. Her apartment once belonged to a Cavalier poet from the seventeenth century. "Gather rosebuds while you may and while you're young go marry, for having once lost your prime, you may forever tarry."

GILLIAN. *(Reciting her lines)* Where was I? Oh yes. "You were supposed to take them with your milk—"

DALE. *(To GILLIAN)* Do you want me to do your chart?

GILLIAN. No! I need to concentrate. *(Grabs stomach)* Ugh. I've got these awful cramps.

DALE. You want a heating pad? Something to drink? A Coke?

GILLIAN. Get away.

DALE. I want to help—

BLAINE. *(Removes headsets. Shows her some pictures in his textbook)* Here, sugar. Did you know the cure for a jellyfish is to pour vinegar on the tentacles? Don't pull them off because they release the poison. If a brown recluse spider bites you, it can kill you. See the fiddle on its back? A black widow, you spot that, you better squash it.

DALE. Oh. No. Stop. *(Crying)* I'm an Aquarius. We're the sign of the most emotion. I feel for others you see. I believe in non-injury to living things so they can roam free.

GILLIAN. *(Puts in some ear plugs)* Time for ear plugs. Where was I ? "Supposed to take them with your milk after breakfast—"

(SOUND: Police whistles scream, announcing a parade.)

DALE. *(To BLAINE)* Parade's coming! Let's take a break.

BLAINE. I've got exams the Monday after Mardi Gras—

DALE. I could give you a quiz on the way to the parade. Make you recite all the ways to die from poison.

BLAINE. I've got those big tests coming up. Remember?

DALE. At least look at your chart? Astrology shows you how to realize the potential genius of yourself. I'm Aquarius with a moon in Virgo, and you're Virgo with a moon in Pisces.

GILLIAN. Quiet—

DALE. I've studied your horoscope and it's what one would call a "fortunate" chart.

GILLIAN. *(Memorizing)* "After your breakfast." No. After your lunch. "After your lunch."

DALE. *(To BLAINE)* You'll always be able to get whatever money you need, and you'll be protected from the worst life can throw at you. For you have the sun in Virgo and the moon in Pisces. Johann Wolfgang von Goethe, born in 1749, had the sun in Virgo and Count Tolstoy, born in 1828, had the moon in Pisces. Moon in Pisces means the aim of your life is to be in tune with the infinite.

GILLIAN. She puts me in a state—

DALE. Something of the magician hovers about you.

GILLIAN. With all the unnecessary useless banter.

DALE. For you've a guardian angel, at your side. And she will give you the power over the world that the magic lamp gave to Aladdin.

(SOUND: Sirens blare outside as a parade approaches.)

GILLIAN. Shut up!

DALE. You ruined my reading. I don't like living with you.

GILLIAN. Blaine, do something.
BLAINE. It's so exhausting—

DALE. *(To* **GILLIAN***)* Stay in your room.

BLAINE. To have to be an evangelist.

DALE. Witch.

GILLIAN. She's off on a rage again.

DALE. Gillian's so mean.

GILLIAN. You hear her, Blaine?

BLAINE. *(Packing his books)* I'm looking for quiet.

GILLIAN. When I've suffered the—

BLAINE. The quiet I can't get.

GILLIAN. The degradation of a sister-in-law who's a loose cannon. Oh, my stomach hurts. Your sister's constantly misbehaving. She's a worthless—restless anxious—being—Oh, my stomach hurts so bad. Ah. Oh.

DALE. She's showing off.

GILLIAN. My period's so screwed up.

BLAINE. Lie down.

DALE. She wants attention.

GILLIAN. Oh. These cramps.

DALE. Last chance for an Oscar.

BLAINE. Is that blood?

GILLIAN. God. Help me.

BLAINE. Get a towel.

DALE. Where?
BLAINE. There. Call an ambulance.

GILLIAN. I can't stop the bleeding.

BLAINE. A damn ambulance.

(SOUND: A band blares as a parade marches down the street.)

DALE. The streets are roped off. A parade's coming.

(end of Act One)

ACT TWO

SCENE 1

(Two months later. A rainy Saturday in May. The living room and bedroom of the apartment. Antique timepieces, stopped at the hour of James Ashton's death, lend the rooms a sweet poignancy. The living room has been made into a sickroom for **DALE**. *White sheets cover the chaise and furniture and her astrology and drawing supplies are everywhere. The bedroom is* **GILLIAN**'s *retreat, where, threatened with miscarriage, she spends most of her time in bed.* **DALE**, *in a long lace nightgown, is bedded in the living room. She acts slow and nervous, as if drugged.* **GILLIAN**, *glamorously disheveled, in a long satin gown, balances a looseleaf checkbook on her bed. She is surrounded by ice cream, Cokes, and champagne. Both women look as if they could be in the medieval gowns of maidens in a golden castle.* **BLAINE** *has just finished replacing his father's portrait over the mantle with one of Gillian on her wedding day. He picks up a cake and crosses to* **DALE**.*)*

BLAINE. Come wish Gillian "Happy Birthday."

DALE. I'm too depressed! I'm sixteen, and I've never seriously accomplished anything.

BLAINE. The Mozart Complex. I've chocolate chip mint ice cream. You ever notice how ice cream shrinks from being a mountain to being a puddle? You get it, and it's gone.

DALE. You don't care how I feel.

BLAINE. You need to get up, move around some.

DALE. I'm too weak.

BLAINE. Learn to trust yourself. It's like someone with an injured leg. If you remain bedridden, your muscles will atrophy. Instead, you must learn to limp by building strength gradually.

DALE. I feel bad about feeling bad but—I can't help it.

BLAINE. Let's wish Gillian happy birthday together.

DALE. You do it.

(BLAINE exits to the bedroom and DALE picks up the phone. The following scenes overlap with DALE talking on the phone and BLAINE tending to GILLIAN.)

BLAINE. Happy birthday to you. Happy birthday to you. Happy birthday, dear Gillian.

GILLIAN. *(Smiles)* I celebrate birthdays, but I don't count them.

BLAINE. You get prettier every day.

GILLIAN. Men say that, but they use age as a standard of decline. *(Her hands run restlessly over her drink.)* No one says I want you to meet my pretty, old wife.

(DALE picks up her cordless phone, dials, and speaks into the phone.)

DALE. Aunt Sara. It's me. I feel sick.

BLAINE. *(Putting a hand on GILLIAN's shoulder)* Make a wish and blow.

DALE. *(Into the phone)* Blaine and Gillian won't come out of their room. And I'm so hot.

BLAINE. What did you wish for?

GILLIAN. A boy.

DALE. *(Into the phone)* I think I've a fever.

BLAINE. I can't manage a baby.

GILLIAN. I know, but if there's any chance for me to carry a baby—that specialist says it's now.

DALE. *(Into the phone)* Blaine and Gillian are doing things.

BLAINE. And what about your career?

DALE. I can hear them panting.

GILLIAN. I didn't think I could get pregnant. The doctors said it was impossible, but I've almost made it to the three-month mark.

DALE. *(Into the phone)* My head hurts.

GILLIAN. I'm so thrilled. Maybe there's a chance for me to be a mom. To make us a family. To grow us closer together.

BLAINE. The doctor says there's a strong possibility you'll still miscarry.

GILLIAN. Don't talk that way about Boo.

BLAINE. What?

GILLIAN. I've named the baby, and I talk to it.

DALE. *(Into the phone)* I'll try, but I don't think I can sleep. Bye. *(Hangs up and starts falling asleep)*

GILLIAN. The doctor said getting pregnant's the hardest thing.

BLAINE. He also said there was an eighty percent chance you'd still lose the baby.

GILLIAN. Well, I've given you permission to be the glum one in this relationship, so we're moving along quite rapidly. You mustn't watch me all the time. It makes me nervous.

BLAINE. How are you feeling?

GILLIAN. You mean how's the spotting? *(Harshly)* Why do you ask that? Less, I think. I mean, who ever says more? I present myself as an example—If you have any serious aspirations about the value of rest. The blood's dark red. So, I guess it's old blood, not...I'm not up to talking about it. I'm full of nervousness.

BLAINE. Let me do the worrying. I've the number for the ambulance right here in case the bleeding gets worse while I'm away. And you have my cell phone number.

GILLIAN. Are you leaving?

BLAINE. Thought I'd catch a couple of hours at the library while you try to nap. You need to rest.

GILLIAN. *(She gets up uneasily, pours more champagne)* I didn't sleep with that downpour last night. No, I didn't. I'm scared to close my eyes. Sometimes I lie here, throat tight, heart pounding, waiting. Then, the room lightens, the air feels thinner, and I know it's morning. These bad nights have made me anxious.

BLAINE. With that new hormone treatment, the spotting could stop completely. If you remain calm.

GILLIAN. But what are those pills doing to me? My hair's falling out. What's wrong? Why are you looking at me?

BLAINE. *(Wipes her brow)* If I look at you, it's to admire how pretty you look.

GILLIAN. My hair was thicker once. Don't you remember? Now when I comb it, I lose a clump.

BLAINE. Your agent called. When you're feeling better, she wants you to try doing voice-overs.

GILLIAN. I've lost the desire to act now that they've fired me from the series. Only one percent of the roles are for women over thirty-five. And if you become pregnant, they send your character to Australia. I don't think anyone gets used to rejection. An actor has to obey all these klutzes. The last two plays I've seen, actors have been completely nude. It's so degrading. I ask myself, "Do I want a part that bad?" Once you start telling a director what you will or won't do, you become a "diva" whom nobody wants. You can't audition with a lousy attitude. You've got to be up, positive. Besides, all the major roles are cast out of New York. My agent thinks I should move.

*(Next door, **DALE** dials them on her portable phone. The phone rings by the bed. **BLAINE** waits uneasily for **GILLIAN** to get it.)*

BLAINE. Let me fluff your pillow.

GILLIAN. Don't fuss about me.

BLAINE. *(With nervous exasperation)* Tell me what you need to feel good, and I'll do it.

GILLIAN. Help me balance the checkbook. We're spending more than we're depositing.

BLAINE. I can't face it. I was in pharmacology class, and I'd stopped taking notes—worrying about you and our finances till I heard the class laughing. The professor had called on me three times. Like the way I felt in Gross Anatomy, when I looked around the room and saw the other kids working on their cadavers—knowing exactly what to do, while I experienced a queasy sensation of total ignorance.

GILLIAN. I don't see how we can afford these doctor bills.

(The phone stops ringing. BLAINE sits to eat cake when DALE again phones them from next door. After 8 rings, BLAINE grabs the phone, and GILLIAN retreats into her champagne.)

BLAINE. *(Into the phone upstage)* Hello.

GILLIAN. If that's Dale, tell her the Waterman pen she gave me leaks.

DALE. *(Into the phone)* You promised to read to me.

GILLIAN. From now on let me sign checks with a cheap pen.

BLAINE. *(Into the phone)* I've got to study.

GILLIAN. *(Watching him jealously)* Who's on the phone?

BLAINE. Wrong number.

GILLIAN. Why does wrong number call so much?

BLAINE. It's Dale. I was joking.

DALE. *(Into the phone)* You can work in my room.

BLAINE. Not today. *(He hangs up. DALE hangs up.)*

GILLIAN. *(Throws the checkbook aside)* Must she keep phoning you?

BLAINE. She's sick, and I'm her brother.

GILLIAN. Why don't you go away with Dale?

BLAINE. *(Clears throat)* Getting mad at Dale won't make you feel better. *(Swallows)* She knows you come first. Look, I'm going to the library.

GILLIAN. Already? It's no fun being married to a dictionary.

BLAINE. *(Checks his watch)* It's getting late.

GILLIAN. At least when Dale was well, there was someone to scream at.

BLAINE. What time is it?

GILLIAN. Who knows? Dale's set your dad's clocks to the hour of his death.

BLAINE. *(Grabs one)* You don't want 'em. I'll throw them out! You think I like to sit up all night memorizing names of bacteria and diseases? I'd rather be dead. But I do it. I buoy myself with caffeine and I do it. It's a lot easier to slug about. *(Tosses the clock)*

GILLIAN. Don't...

BLAINE. You smile, maybe for a sentence, or in bed and poof like a match, you're out. It's not a relationship when you're living with Mrs. Gloom. It's not just the speaking; I need a happy face. And then when I hear you whine, "I'm so depressed," I think how lucky the garbage men are. They drive by, unload the dumpster, and drive on. The trick is to keep you from dumping. If throwing out the clocks will do it, let's kill the clocks. *(Dumps another clock)* Christ. What's gotten into me. *(With a nervous panic)* God, I'm sorry. I—

GILLIAN. *(Her eyes meet his.)* You do pretty well—being married to a phantom.

BLAINE. I'm sorry. It's just that...I'm so wound up, I forgot your surprise— *(Scoops her up and carries her to the doorway)* I always wanted a portrait of you over the mantle, so—Happy Birthday. It's a good likeness, don't you think? The day you look your prettiest, your wedding.

GILLIAN. And your funeral. This must have cost a fortune.

BLAINE. You're worth it.

GILLIAN. Look, one eye's lit up, one's dark.

BLAINE. You look like this nineteenth-century princess.

GILLIAN. The color of my hair is all wrong.

BLAINE. *(Carrying her back to the bed)* You've the hands of royalty—long and narrow. God, you're beautiful. Expressive eyes, that ethereal smile.

GILLIAN. *(Unzips her gown)* Are you lusting after me?

(DALE begins rocking back and forth.)

BLAINE. It's the gown. The way you unzip it. It was like John Singer Sargent. It had a nice rustle to it. *(They kiss.)* Kissing you reminds me of what a miracle the human body is.

GILLIAN. Lock the door. Didn't your daddy tell you about bad girls?

BLAINE. I'm a dead man's son. I make up the rules. I'm going to dance around you. Like a moth round a fire. Give myself over to chaos.

*(Lights fade as **BLAINE** crawls into bed with **GILLIAN**.)*

SCENE 2

(Later that evening. **GILLIAN** *stands on a chair, adjusting her portrait.* **DALE** *watches, staring.)*

DALE. Is Blaine never coming home?

GILLIAN. He'll be back when he's done studying. *(Beat)* Papa's been deposed.

DALE. *(To* **GILLIAN***)* You don't have to feel bad about not wanting me here. I know I'm moody. My moon is in Virgo, so it's no wonder I'm Byronic.

GILLIAN. It's so difficult right now.

DALE. If you let me, I could help...

GILLIAN. I've the number of the doctor right here. *(Leans back slowly)* God, I've a headache. You can't know what it's like for us to keep going.

DALE. 'Course I do. I'm trying to live my life completely from love—

GILLIAN. Well, back off a bit.

DALE. I got your birthday gift at a little shop in the shadow of the Cathedral.

GILLIAN. *(Lifts up a crystal ball)* My, it's heavy.

DALE. It's a gazing ball. It reflects the moon and the planets. If you touch it, and meditate, the quality of your prayer will shoot up to a new level.

GILLIAN. It's chilly.

DALE. The ball can't feel weather. It's always cold.

GILLIAN. Too bad.

DALE. Lift it. The gazing ball is pink now, but it'll turn blue, lilac, and gold. In the daylight, one half of the ball is dark. Light has the same energy as love. It's true. Southerners are a people of the sun. We used to be a people of the moon, we let the stars rule us, and we watched the moonlight. Then people lived in small places between the earth and sky. God was in the sky, man was on earth, and love was the link between the two. Make a wish. Close your eyes and bare your soul.

GILLIAN. I feel quietly exalted.

DALE. I'd love to do your chart. I believe the spirit's older than the body, and if you tap the soul of another person, the body will revive. I'm resuscitating various parts of myself, opening up drawers, seeing what's there. I want you to know how much being here means to me.

GILLIAN. I do, but—your living here complicates things.

DALE. I would live with y'all anywhere...I've been reading the mystic Schaeffer, who accepts people as they are.

GILLIAN. It's too crowded. Charts and markers all about.

DALE. I could move by the washroom. I'm like jello. You can put me anywhere. I guess Blaine told you...I've this hole in my heart. I'll probably never get married. I've already lived more than they said I would and—*(Breathes heavily)* All I need is my little duck and these snapshots. You can throw the rest of my stuff out.

GILLIAN. Blaine needs quiet.

DALE. Don't lie. You don't like me living here. Sometimes, I put photos around the room, and pretend that I'm back home.

GILLIAN. I don't want to be a deliberate loser, but you're going to have to move.

DALE. *(Pulling out a knife)* Other times, I run this knife over my wrists—telling myself to simply end life.

GILLIAN. Give me the knife.

DALE. You think I don't exist as a feeling person.

GILLIAN. Hand it over.

DALE. I'm terrified I'm going to say something wrong, and that I should cut my tongue out.

GILLIAN. What are you doing?

DALE. I'd like to...rip your picture. Let you see what pain looks like. I know I can't please you. I'm stupid. Oh my! *(Runs wailing to the bathroom)*

GILLIAN. *(Running after her, banging on bathroom door)* Dale! Dale! Dale!...

SCENE 3

(DALE is in her daybed, GILLIAN is resting in her room, and BLAINE is in the kitchen. SARA arrives, bedecked in Oscar de la Renta and carrying champagne, chocolates, and ladyfingers. A thunderstorm rages outside. SARA opens the door with a key.)

SARA. Yoo hoo. Anybody home? I've got champagne and chocolates. It's fine to have an apartment over Jackson Square, but at least install an elevator. There's nothing but ignorance in the Quarter. What a dramatic sky. Rain everywhere, and no one's using umbrellas. The sky is like sharks' teeth. There's a woman out front with a broom. She sits under the gallery but does nothing. I said to her, "Why don't you at least sweep?" *(Removes and shakes out her raincoat)* You're all alone?

DALE. They're around. I was dreaming that y'all were burying me—

SARA. How can you ever improve if—

DALE. Under the James Ashton tree.

SARA. You don't stop the morbidity.

DALE. There's so much shade there...'cause that tree's really two trunks...that grew together. I flew to the treetop.

SARA. They should let some light in here.

DALE. *(Breathing heavily)* From there, the graveyard looked so sweet. The graves were white-washed and numbered. Some names plates had faded—

SARA. Don't talk.

DALE. I spotted some Agapanthus, Dad's favorite flower. The more they're crushed together, the happier they are...And pyracanthus. They're supposed to do well in northern climates, but for some reason they thrive here.

SARA. *(Touches DALE's forehead)* You're in a cold sweat.

DALE. I met Uncle Otto with his dog, Rip. And picked some oleanders—

SARA. *(Throws her hat off)* That's enough! Quiet!

DALE. What's wrong with your face?

SARA. Worry. Grief. What else? *(Rises abruptly, marches to the bedroom, and raps on the door)* Yoo-hoo. *(Hurts her knuckles, examines them)*

| **BLAINE.** | **SARA.** | **GILLIAN.** |
| One minute. | I'm in a yucky mood. | This is a bad time... |

SARA. I could gobble everyone up.

(BLAINE enters. While he, SARA, and DALE talk, GILLIAN fixes up and changes into a long crimson at-home gown.)

BLAINE. Keep your voice down. Ssh. Let's go onto the balcony—

SARA. How about a kiss? My nephew doesn't even know who I am. I have to introduce myself on the way in.

BLAINE. You should call before you barge over.

SARA. I don't think nephews ever pay you back for what you did right.

BLAINE. Over here.

SARA. You can't plan a life and say if I only do things that are high-minded, my family will admire me. They hate you anyway if you keep traveling to Paris.

BLAINE. I've not much to say to you after you—

SARA. Don't punish me for your bad marks.

BLAINE. You ruined my honeymoon!

SARA. I was operating in the best interests of the—

BLAINE. Spare me.

SARA. *(Sniffs back a tear)* Life has got to mean more than a honeymoon, a degree, or even your nephew insulting you.

BLAINE. You'd better go. *(Looking out)* Where's Joe?

SARA. Who? Gone for a ham sandwich and won't be back.

BLAINE. You drove?

SARA. You can't get killed in my Cadillac. Trains get out of the way.

BLAINE. *(Getting her coat)* Let me get your wrap.

SARA. *(Skirting him)* Blaine's such a gentleman. He'll be fighting with you, but he'll help you with your coat. It's that woman who's turned you against me.

BLAINE. Gillian has influenced me, yes. It's because of her, I'm letting you—

SARA. *(Pouting)* Aren't you going to ask me, "How was Paris?"

BLAINE. How was Paris?

SARA. Brilliant one minute. Boring the next—

DALE. *(Rising slowly)* Let me take your hat. Is that lipstick on your cheek?

SARA. It comes and goes. My nephew says it's my meanness popping out. *(Gestures to* **DALE***)* Put on your robe and slippers.

DALE. Which ones? I don't know what season it is. I sort of drift through the universe.

SARA. The child suffers from neglect. She's stopped eating and batters me with phone calls. *(To* **BLAINE***)* Are you making your classes?

BLAINE. I go to class. Any class after eleven, I'm there.

SARA. You're failing. Your body can't keep up with your mind. You look awful. Bags under the eyes. Your skin's sallow—How many articles have you published? None? Blaine had fourteen articles published by twenty-one, Dale. He was our shooting star. In February, he barely passed his combined tests.

*(He stares at **SARA** contemptuously, then turns his eyes toward the door as if he fears **GILLIAN** is coming.)*

BLAINE. I wanted to take a leave, but Gillian wouldn't have it. I've been studying a lot...over the past few days.

SARA. Do you have a nervous condition? Speaking in bursts.

BLAINE. I'd like to hear you out, but—

SARA. Boys raised in an elegant household can be highly vulnerable. How's Gillian?

BLAINE. I'm sure Dale told you.

SARA. She lies on the couch eating chocolates and turning into the great white blimp. I'd take any spouse, even a blimp, but there aren't too many tall, good-looking men left. There're not too many short ugly ones either.

BLAINE. She's pregnant.

SARA. I know.

BLAINE. And the baby's in trouble.

SARA. She's too old.

BLAINE. Doc Ryan says Gillian needs absolute calm.

*(**BLAINE** forces his face into a kindly expression. **SARA** examines a plate of ladyfinger cakes.)*

*(**GILLIAN** enters, tipsy, in a red dress. She holds a glass of champagne which she has been guzzling. She gives **BLAINE** a nervous look, her manner self-conscious. **BLAINE** grows increasingly agitated with **GILLIAN**'s drinking.)*

GILLIAN. What about Doc Ryan?

BLAINE. You should be resting.

GILLIAN. *(Gestures to the portrait)* I wanted to see y'all's reaction to my birthday gift. Well, what do you think?

DALE. That picture's so...peculiar.

SARA. It does capture a certain "*Je ne sais quoi.*" Perfect for over a casket in a funeral parlor.

GILLIAN. Or over a mantle in the Baroness de Pontalba's apartment.

SARA. You've gotten so pale. And puffy.

GILLIAN. Arthritis—

SARA. I never knew what arthritis was till I was forty. Men do need a fecund woman coming from good stock.

GILLIAN. *(To* **SARA***)* What a fancy outfit.

SARA. I worked with my designer to "do" this dress. Oscar won't design for anyone who won't wear him exclusively, so I had to throw out all my clothes—you want his number?

GILLIAN. *(Starts to pass her and stumbles, a bit tipsy)* I didn't say I liked it. I said it was fancy— *(Dryly)* Actually I do...like it. Let's open the champagne.

BLAINE. *(To* **GILLIAN***, regarding the champagne)* Careful. I love your dress.

GILLIAN. I got tired of all that black. With Blaine gone all the time, the neighbors thought I was a widow. So I went and bought a scarlet dress in a miracle fabric.

SARA. Let's prudently change the subject.

GILLIAN. I've been putting up with you damned people...trying to create a personal life. But you're like bats; as soon as I get rid of one of you, another one flies in through the belfry.

DALE. I'm praying for you. That you'll find the courage to risk letting God in your life.

GILLIAN. I know about your spirituality. Fanaticism sometimes used to counteract a charmlessness in a person. Some people make themselves more intrusive than anyone thought they'd be.

DALE. *(Sobbing)* Oh my...Oh my.

SARA. The girl is grieving.

GILLIAN. I'm trying to dislocate the sensor that makes me resent the hell out of you.

BLAINE. *(To* **GILLIAN***)* Honey, you've got to rest.

GILLIAN. Later.

SARA. Since Dale's moved here, her new doctor says she sleepwalks at night. I talked to Dr. Ryan on the phone. The man's more radical, but somehow sincere.

DALE. All of a sudden I feel this presence. Like someone is in the room. *(She races to the bathroom.)*

SARA. Midnight ravings, and the doctor's prescribing more antidepressants for her mood swings. He can't figure out why Dale's running a low-grade fever. It's more than the shock of her father's death; they know that much now. He feels Dale isn't being appropriately monitored, and that Gillian isn't sensitive to her condition. I'll stay with you for a few days. Access the situa—

GILLIAN. Ah-ha! There's the hitch. I don't want family snoops. *(Waves of anxiety rush through her. She grasps her stomach.)*

BLAINE. Will you get in bed?

GILLIAN. *(To* **SARA***)* You invade my house. Come barging in and think you can do that.

BLAINE. Aunt Sara was leaving.

GILLIAN. *(To* **SARA***)* You're a neurotic criminal. A swindler with no sense of consequence. Casting a spell by disapproving of me. I've a right to my own body, my own privacy. *(She clutches her stomach.)* Ah. Ooh!

SARA. Tut. Tut. Sick people, they use up the living.

BLAINE. *(To* **GILLIAN***)* Why must you punish me? Let's go to the bedroom.

GILLIAN. No.

SARA. No. I must talk to you. I bought y'all a house. It's one of those marvelous Gothic Revival houses. Delicate in appearance in this soft, rose shade. The style takes its inspiration from twelfth-century cathedrals. With pointed arches, and diamond-shaped lights. And it's on St. Charles Avenue.

GILLIAN. *(To* **SARA***)* Near your house?

SARA. Down the block. Blaine used to make his nurse pass it. So I said to myself, why not buy the boy something?

GILLIAN. But I like this apartment!

SARA. Surely you want what's best for Blaine—The boy's exhausted. I can't in good conscience watch you both flounder.

BLAINE. It's stupid to imagine awful things, but I worry when I leave—

SARA. If you were nearby, the servants could help out.

GILLIAN. I'm not moving.

SARA. *(Takes a sandwich)* Since y'all married, I've been poised for catastrophe.

BLAINE. We don't have to make a decision right away.

SARA. *(Screams offstage)* Dale.

GILLIAN. She's in the bathroom.

BLAINE. *(To* **SARA***)* Get her. I need to talk to Gillian alone.

SARA. I'm starving. Where's your kitchen? *(Exits)*

BLAINE. *(To* **GILLIAN***)* You should eat. I don't get it. What's so horrible about her buying us a house?

GILLIAN. I want to live uptown, I do, but when I think of them next door, I hyperventilate.

BLAINE. *(Passes her the contract)* The contract's already been signed.

GILLIAN. Interesting. Ha, ha! The house was bought for you and your sister. See your names and Social Security numbers here.

BLAINE. A formality. Aunt Sara has seen so many marriages fail, she doesn't count on—

GILLIAN. Ours to last.

BLAINE. I'm sorry my family's so screwy. I was born into an insane asylum; I got out.

GILLIAN. *(GILLIAN clasps her stomach and moans.)* Ooh.

BLAINE. God, no—

GILLIAN. I've known women like your aunt.

BLAINE. Sit. Oh, please—

GILLIAN. Egomaniacs living for themselves—

BLAINE. Gillian, please—

GILLIAN. They destroy their in-laws' lives...because nobody stops them. *(Grabs her stomach)* Ooh. Ah.

BLAINE. It's going to be all right. I'm here.

GILLIAN. The new wife hopes she can make it because the sex is good, and the sister's spells of brooding are short. I want to destroy this paper.

BLAINE. Yes. Yes. What is it? Are you bleeding badly?

GILLIAN. I lived with bullies like your aunt. Wouldn't buy you a house—but where they wanted it. They need a man to control because they're out of control themselves.

BLAINE. Look, I just talked to her. Rest for a while, eat something.

GILLIAN. Talking to your aunt doesn't work because the woman lies. And you? You believe her excuses.

BLAINE. Close your eyes for a second. It'll do you a world of good. When Dad died, I was practically crazy with loneliness. He died three times—wiped out totally—but the doctors kept bringing him back. But then he was gone, see. Really dead. I was shaking in my shoes for weeks, shaking like a little hard stone. I put myself in a situation in my classes where I had to work at a speed that allowed no time for sadness. I had my family and my studies, but was constantly lonely. And then I met you. And I had this awakening experience. Just being near you I feel this burst of energy around my heart like it's all white, exploding full of love. Unconditional love. That's why I can love you as I do and Dale at the same time.

GILLIAN. Do you think we could live far away, after med school?

BLAINE. Trouble is, you grow up in New Orleans and you like to have it around. I could compromise. *(BLAINE looks grimly away and walks to the window.* **GILLIAN** *runs her fingers nervously over her stomach.)* I know I shouldn't trust Aunt Sara, but the situation here isn't working. I'd like to hire a companion for Dale. Pay for her to see the best specialists and for you to—But what will I use for money? Move to that house for a year. For the love of Jesus, let's do this.

GILLIAN. I was so fit before this—You remember. Making love with you night after night. When the doctor told me I couldn't have kids, I handled it. But when I found out I was pregnant, I felt young again. Like a teenager. I want Boo to live, Blaine. I want to be a family. I can't live by your relatives. I feel myself disintegrating when they're around.

BLAINE. Listen, Gillian. I want a family more than anything. But why can't you accept that Dale is part of our family? *(Clears throat. Pulls out a report)* Dale is just having problems creating a new structure for herself. Her medication works, but only for a period of time.

GILLIAN. Oh Lord, don't—

BLAINE. Dale's got to continue living with us—here or in that house.

GILLIAN. Won't your aunt take care of Dale?

BLAINE. She's not going to care for my sister alone. She's never had to do anything alone, and she's not going to start now. If Dale is near us, I can keep an eye on her. Why are you against living uptown? We'll have our own house. You don't have to go to their—

GILLIAN. I've sympathy for your sister, but you made a promise to me. I see myself getting sicker every day. And if I lose the baby, it'll be your fault.

BLAINE. Don't say that. Can't you see? I'm desperate, exhausted. Dale's in a very heightened state. It's a restorative measure the body is taking on for—

GILLIAN. I'm not moving.

BLAINE. That's it? You're going to leave me...hanging? You go do any nasty thing you like. It's pretty horrible to...Dale's young.

GILLIAN. And I'm not.

BLAINE. She has feelings, for God's sake.

GILLIAN. And I don't.

BLAINE. You want me to pretend she hasn't suffered shock.

GILLIAN. My first husband was a stuntman. Caught on fire, jumped off cliffs. He was a man who punished you when you said "No." Once my husband got so mad, he cracked an egg on my head. Another time, he busted my lip. See, here's the scar. The day I left him, he held a gun to my head and screamed, "I'm going to kill you." *(GILLIAN's speech accelerates. Thunder crashes.)* See where he put out a cigarette in my scalp? Do you know what it's like not to be able to sleep because your heart is racing so fast? To have this permanent shakiness in your fingers? *(She grasps her stomach as if she's just had a cramp.)* I spent my marriage forgetting details of events that took place hours before. Wore turtlenecks to cover the bruises. After I found the guts to leave him, I never let fear stop me like it did before. And now my body's alive again, and I'll do anything to keep our baby.

BLAINE. I'm sure Dale's condition will improve...if we move her. God, I'm betting it will.

GILLIAN. Do as you like. Send her to your aunt's, to boarding school, to the hospital. Feel free to live with Dale if you want. But I will not. I've got to rest.

*(***GILLIAN** *starts to exit.)*

BLAINE. I taught her how to walk, how to tie her shoe. How to flatten a penny on the tracks.

*(***GILLIAN** *exits.* **BLAINE** *picks up a medical book, skims it, hurls it down. Stuffs the contract in his pocket. Blues music drifts up from the street. He walks out onto the balcony as* **SARA** *enters looking for* **BLAINE** *with chocolates and some liqueur glasses.)*

SARA. Cabernet Sauvignon?

BLAINE. Here. On the balcony. Gillian's gone to bed. She's very edgy. She needs rest, but she can't rest.

SARA. It's difficult to control someone you care about.

BLAINE. Will you stop?

SARA. She's an actress! The stage is her God.

BLAINE. She's quit acting.

SARA. Chocolate?

BLAINE. Thanks.

SARA. Chocolate should be enjoyed with a dessert wine. Look outside at the light and the land. Dale says light defines experience but I think it's the land. Jackson Square. Your sister's in the bathroom sobbing.

BLAINE. There's no heros in the real world, just in bad fiction. You're going to have to hire someone to live with her in that house.

SARA. A stranger. When she has a brother?

BLAINE. Then you'll have to take her back in. *(Calls)* Dale, come here.

DALE. *(Offstage)* Coming.

SARA. *(Reaches for a drink)* I can't handle it. Her willful attempts to get attention, the suicide threats. The trigger can be almost anything—ice, an unexpected rainstorm. Look, I've chewed my lips so bad, they're bleeding. Thank God for Drambuie.

BLAINE. Are you going to numb yourself to sleep?

SARA. They say if there's no support structure at home, she'll have to learn limits inside a clinic. Of course, they do have that adolescent program at De Paul, but it's all so humiliating.

BLAINE. I can't toss her in a bin with the freaks. I've worried about Dale so much longer than you. Since she was born.

SARA. At seventeen, she'll need to go to the adult ward. Then Dr. Ryan talks about some experimental studies with needle electrodes...that have a higher response rate than drug therapy.

DALE. Y'all, it's so exciting. *(Runs in)* A bat's on the ledge by the window.

BLAINE. Calm down.

DALE. I cracked the door, and when I went to open it, that bat's pointed face looked up at me with its wings fanned out.

SARA. Don't buzz about me.

DALE. I once had two bats in my room. I woke up one night to this whirl flying about. When I saw it was a bat, I scrunched under the covers.

SARA. Stop emoting.

DALE. The next day, Daddy died. Are bats a sign of death?

BLAINE. I don't know. Dale, listen. Gillian and I may not be moving to that...house on Saint Charles.

DALE. But Aunt Sara's already bought it.

BLAINE. Gillian likes it here.

DALE. If only you'd show it to her, she'd be mad for that big house. It has a side entrance—under a *porte cochere*. There's a room with a view of a garden with a kind of early evening dark. She'll have such energy in that house.

BLAINE. I'm upset about it—

SARA. *(To BLAINE)* Blaine's upset, but not so upset it galvanizes him to compassion. Gillian will change her mind. Take your time and seize the right opportunity to show her the house. To catch prey, leopards lie in wait in tree branches. When the animal passes below, the cat pounces on it.

BLAINE. *(To DALE)* You think you'd like us all in that house, but you wouldn't if—Have you never felt bad about hanging around married people so much?

GILLIAN. *(Offstage)* Blaine!

(BLAINE exits)

DALE. It's Gillian who's poisoned...him...against me.

SARA. I've got to go to *les toilettes*.

(SARA exits. DALE gasps and wails after them.)

DALE. Gillian lies because she wants...Blaine for herself— I've tried to reach her. But I can't. She's so cold, vultures get out of her way.

(A tropical storm descends. Thunder, lightning and darkness. DALE gets a suitcase out of the hall closet and begins collecting pictures, paperweights. Her nervous state is extremely apparent. She is a young girl who has cracked up before and is going to crack again—perhaps repeatedly. DALE's eyes dart away, picking objects out of the gloom. The scene is bathed in a deep silver, almost bluish light; the heavy furniture gleams with dampness from the rain outside.)

GILLIAN. Lightning hit the balcony.

DALE. *(Tossing objects in the suitcase)* Blaine's losing it. Screaming because I want to...live near...you. I can't stand y'all...I'm taking my basket. My picture. My tray.

GILLIAN. You feel helpless?

DALE. I'm going away. Where's that locket of my baby hair and my picture— Blaine kept on the mantle?

(GILLIAN clutches the back of a chair and draws a few deep breaths as if she had sudden cramps. DALE gasps for breath.)

DALE. If I thought Blaine would never see me again, I'd set my body on fire, burn myself up. Might as well talk about the clinic...People telling me not to do what I want to do, not to feel what I can't help feeling. Worry eating me alive.

GILLIAN. Love Blaine, but let him have his own life.

DALE. I'm not taking it from him!

GILLIAN. What am I supposed to do—Forget that I'm married?

DALE. I want my gazing ball back.

GILLIAN. Never lead an adult life—

(DALE grabs a suitcase and tosses the ball in, yanks down some clocks.)
DALE. And Daddy's clocks. On any one night he'd have forty clocks ticking in the house. This picture of Blaine belongs to me.

GILLIAN. I know it's difficult for you...

DALE. Half of that big house was mine. You wouldn't have had to see me.

GILLIAN. You've got to accept certain unpleasant things about Blaine and me, that we're married and want to be alone. I failed so miserably before—

DALE. I'm taking my baby cup Blaine was keeping. These bronzed baby shoes. And this locket of hair. *(DALE runs to the door, but GILLIAN seizes her by the wrist.)* Oh, I can't breathe.

GILLIAN. Blaine's the first decent thing in my life—

DALE. I knew what you were from the first. Taking everything for yourself and…I'm running away—

GILLIAN. It's not normal how you cling to Blaine.

DALE. I'm never coming back.

GILLIAN. Whenever you're in the room, I look up and I see you either glaring or gazing at him. You don't want him to be happy because you want him scared, hopeless, shaken to the bone. It's a lifestyle I won't move into. I won't let you jump, hop, and scurry your way into my life.

(GILLIAN forces DALE to her knees, crying hysterically.)

DALE. I've a right to my own brother. Get away. Back off. You witch! I'll hurt you if you don't let me live here. You want to get rid of me? Why don't you kill me? *(Takes a knife and pushes it in GILLIAN's hand)* Hurry up and get it over with. Kill me!

(Entering, his face haggard, BLAINE pulls them apart. The storm builds outside. The wind over the Mississippi rises, sweeping over Jackson Square. Lightning streaks the sky.)

BLAINE. Gillian!

DALE. She's making up lies about me.

GILLIAN. I'm not!

DALE. *(Her breath quickens.)* It's like this fist's…closing…over my…My heart's pounding, hammering, beating flip-flops.

BLAINE. What have you done to her? She's burning up.

GILLIAN. She's crazy.

GILLIAN. Ah.

DALE. Listen or I'll blow your heads off.

BLAINE. *(Steps forward)* Hand me the gun. I'm walking to you now. If you shoot someone, it'll be me.

DALE. Stay back.

BLAINE. No.

DALE. I'm warning you.

BLAINE. The gun—

DALE. Back or I'll shoot.

BLAINE. Hand it—*(DALE shoots the gun.)* Awl.

SARA. You almost hurt Blaine.

GILLIAN. You nearly killed him.

DALE. It's Gillian's fault. She made me do it.

(She ducks from him, runs into the bedroom, locks the door.)

BLAINE. Dale, open up.

DALE. I'll kill myself. Cause she made me do it.

GILLIAN. Oh, God.

BLAINE. Open the door.

SARA. Oh, please, Dale, please.

(BLAINE breaks down the door as police sirens resound from a distance. DALE is stretched out in a pool of blood. They cross to her moaning, "Oh no. Please. Lord. What did she do?" when DALE jumps up.)

DALE. Surprise! I think I should go on stage with Gillian. You like my death scene? *(Police sirens grow louder out front.)* Fake blood from the magic store. Great joke, ha-ha. I really scared you. Ha.

BLAINE. *(Crosses to the phone and picks up the receiver)* Hello? 911? My sister Dale Ashton has attempted suicide. Could you send someone up? Please contact her doctor. Dr. Howard Ryan at Touro, and have him meet her at the hospital. Then deliver my sister there. *(Gets out suitcase)*

SARA. What are you doing?

BLAINE. Packing. I'm going away. *(To* **GILLIAN***)* You coming?

GILLIAN. With wings. *(Begins to pack)*

SARA. Are you crazy?

BLAINE. Maybe. Buddhists believe great fortune belongs to those who release living things. I release you, Dale. I release you, Sara.

SARA. Don't you care about your sister? She needs—

BLAINE. This time, the authorities will handle the situation.

SARA. The authorities!

BLAINE. Aunt Sara, I'm putting Dale in your capable hands. I know it's going to be a rough time for her, but you can get through it together. You've lived a fearful life, Aunt Sara, now you can come into your own. A wife has to come before a sister. A baby before anyone. I'm leaving for a much needed rest. My wife never had a honeymoon. New Orleans is the city Rhett Butler took Scarlet O'Hara to after their wedding. Bye, Dale.

(They exit)

SARA. *(Screams)* What hotel are you going to? Blaine! Answer me! Tell me!

BLAINE AND GILLIAN. *(Their voices overlap offstage)* We'll call you.

DALE. My heart.

BLAINE. Get her pills.

GILLIAN. Dale, you mustn't pretend.

DALE. This roaring's in my ears.

BLAINE. Put a pillow under her.

DALE. *(Gulps air furiously. Her body stiffens in apprehension.)* Don't leave me, Blaine.

BLAINE. I won't.

DALE. *(To* **GILLIAN***)* Blaine wouldn't have said "no" to that house...if you didn't...hate me.

BLAINE. I didn't say no.

GILLIAN. What did you say?

(SOUND: Thunder crashes.)

DALE. How would you like it if someone threw you away?

GILLIAN. *(Clutches her stomach)* No. Ugh.

BLAINE. You're cramping.

DALE. Faker. I hate your apartment.

BLAINE. *(Leads* **GILLIAN** *to the chaise lounge)* Rest.

DALE. I hope it burns. I hope you burn in hell.

BLAINE. *(The lights flicker and go out.)* Dale. Quiet.

DALE. I hope you lose...everything you love. I hope God kills your baby.

(*BLAINE slaps DALE in the face. He walks slowly and sits by GILLIAN. Rain pours. Lightning flashes. The lights go out. DALE crosses with a candle as if seeking a ghost. Thunder claps and the sound of rain closes in. DALE drifts to the balcony as a diamond-like sheet of rain descends, catching the light and quietly gleaming. DALE extends her hands under the rainfall, turning them as if to cleanse them. Then she scoops up water and cools her forehead. The rainfall increases. DALE takes her hands from her burning forehead and stretches them through the rain as if reaching for someone beyond the moon.*)

DALE. *(To Daddy, laughs)* Daddy. How'd you find me?

BLAINE. Who are you talking to?

DALE. *(To DADDY)* Magic. I'm the empress of Louisiana, remember? *(To BLAINE)* Blaine, that's disgusting. I think most men who desire virgins are insecure about sex. They feel since the girl's never had any, she'll think they're good. My, you're a hustler. Button your shirt up. *(To DADDY)* Go kill me. Get it over with. *(Searches about. DALE grabs SARA's purse. BLAINE starts toward DALE.)*

BLAINE. I don't know how to help you.

DALE. Say your rosary, get in bed. Daddy's come. He's alive. He can come out the grave. Let's take a joyride. *(Exits)*

BLAINE. We've got to catch her.

GILLIAN. *(Blocks the door)* Just trample me down. Hurry up and get it over with.

(SOUND: An alarm blares. Sound of cars braking over a sodden road.)

BLAINE. Move.

GILLIAN. No. If she can't have you, she's going to— put herself in the emergency room. One pays for relatives, if relatives don't learn.

(SOUND: An alarm blares. An engine rushes offstage.)

SARA. *(Running in from the bathroom)* She's gunning my Cadillac like a missile. I saw her from the bathroom window. We'd better go down.

(*SARA exits. BLAINE peers about, wild-eyed. GILLIAN's facial muscles twitch and she draws in her breath with a sharp sound. Picks up the phone. The alarm cuts off.*)

BLAINE. I can't watch her kill herself. Go and identify the body.

GILLIAN. Call the police and her doctor. (*Dials the phone*)

BLAINE. What are you doing?

GILLIAN. Stopping this. (*Into the phone.*) Hello. This is Mrs. Ashton. Could you send...a patrol car over? The Pontalba apartments. Saint Peter. My sister, Dale Ashton is...heading down Chartres Street in a stolen vehicle.

(*GILLIAN drops the receiver and grabs her stomach. Her lips form a mute O. She cannot talk. She stands motionless, breathing heavily. He watches her. Rain pours outside. Lightning flashes.*)

BLAINE. God! Get off your feet. I'll be right back.

GILLIAN. (*She lies down.*) We've got to finish this. I know you've been excessively close to Dale.

BLAINE. Go lie in our room—

GILLIAN. Your long walks. And all those nights you tucked her in bed when your dad was ill.

BLAINE. You think our relationship was as rotten-minded as—All of Dale's problems are related to my father. He worshiped her. It wasn't anything crude and incestuous. Just an aging father loving a pretty daughter who reminded him of his young wife. She reflected his youth back to him like a twisted mirror. And when Dad died, Dale became a sort...of widow.

GILLIAN. Oh, it's so attractive to be a helpless waif buffeted by the seas of an unfair world. Well, the wild ride is finally ended. You have a choice. I know this is painful, but are you going to let her destroy both of you?

(*Sounds of someone running up the stairs.* **SARA** *rushes back in.*)

SARA. Dale's started up my Cadillac. If you care about Dale, don't let her die.

GILLIAN. I wish one of these times she would die. She's inflicted so much pain on Blaine.

SARA. And what have you given Blaine, a barren future.

(DALE charges in, disheveled and muddy, with a gun.)

DALE. That's it. Hands up. Faces to the wall. All of you.

SARA. My gun.

DALE. Going to see if this works.

SARA. Put that down, it's loaded.

BLAINE. Give me the gun.

DALE. Faces to the wall, I said.

(SARA and GILLIAN turn.)

BLAINE. Wait!

DALE. Turn around.

BLAINE. Look—Dale. Hold on a minute.

DALE. I'm racing the engine and I realize it's not me I want to kill. It's her. Her, Aunt Sara, and that baby. Everybody, lie on the floor now.

BLAINE. Don't move, y'all.

DALE. Put your faces on the ground, or I'll shoot. *(Waves the gun around)*

BLAINE. Why are you doing this?

DALE. Drop, I said. *(Shoots the ceiling)* Think you can ignore how I feel? That I'm that dumb? Lie down, bitch.

SARA. Oh.

SCENE FOUR

(A rainy Christmas Eve, seven months later. 6:00 p. m. At rise of curtain, a street version of Jingle Bells resounds, a clock chimes, and Cathedral bells ring out. A bassinet with blue bows dresses one corner. **BLAINE** *hurries in, wearing a raincoat. He unloads snacks: cheese straws, caviar, egg nog, a metallic tree dressed with tinsel and gold babies. He pours himself some egg nog in a mint julep cup and reads a card.)*

BLAINE. *(Drops card and talks to his son)* "Merry Christmas to my Louisiana Gentleman." I am not a Louisiana gentleman. I'm not sure what that is. But if any of the predictions of the doom of my family are true, I want to be there with my own life when my family dies....Last year, when they put your Aunt Dale in the hospital, I lay on the railroad tracks and prayed that a train would hit me. It was pouring outside, just like tonight. I resigned myself to death, and it was easy. I woke up with the sound of fire scorching metal, and walked off the tracks. Most times, fire puts you to sleep....Your Aunt Dale is coming home from DePaul Clinic tonight. That's a place where they fix people who are broken in the head. She's better. Aunt Sara visited her once. She'd go more often, but she remarried and travels a lot. I go twice a week with Dale's dog, Voyager. Woof. Woof. Now and then, Dale looks to see if he's standing up or lying on the ground. Robins have adopted her. She fed them some crumbs and now they peck away. Scratch. Scratch. She says they got those red breasts from picking the nails out of Christ's hands. *(Places some sketches about the room)* Most times I visit, Dale draws and I sit there and listen to the wind chimes ringing out. You can do too much for fear of the need to do something. Drawing's become an obsession. She's done a series of spring dresses. You know the story of Persephone, the goddess of spring? Persephone was condemned to Hades, but Zeus said she could return to earth six months a year, if she could row down the River Styx past her relatives who screamed out for help and not stop. Dale says becoming an adult feels like that.

(SOUND: A pounding on the door.)

BLAINE. Who is it?

SARA. *(Offstage into the intercom)* Mrs. Claus.

BLAINE. You're early, Aunt Sara.

*(***BLAINE** *flattens his hair and opens the door.* **SARA** *enters in a long Christmas gown with an extravagant coat and hat.)*

SARA. Titantic weather. Some woman's walking a duck down the street. There's a drunk by the doorway. A man shooting some film let me in.

BLAINE. Merry Christmas.

SARA. *(Sticking her cheek out for a kiss)* Thank you, darling.

BLAINE. *(Takes her coat and shakes out droplets of water)* Mm. Fabulous coat.

SARA. I dress like I want. I don't owe anybody anything.

(He exits to the kitchen.)

SARA. Where's beauty boy?

BLAINE. *(Offstage)* Asleep.

SARA. Ooh. What an adorable snore. *(Talks to the baby)* For my baby, Saks is delivering three flying monkeys, a teddy bear, and something with tiny feet, a head, and a big spindly back. It looks like a roller toy, but it's an African porcupine. *(Crosses to the door)* Weather's ghastly, somewhere between a mist and a drizzle. You can almost taste that old Creole dust. Driving down here, the traffic was barely creeping, and the wreck was on the other side of the road. *(Waves at the car)* Francois, I'm over here. My husband forgets where you live from trip to trip. We'd come more often but—*(Looking out, screams)* Francois, come inside. The man knows no strangers, because he talks to everyone. Artists. *(Sniffs, calls out to **BLAINE**)* The Quarter is a place I'll never get used to. Rancid odor? I could go all year without smelling that River. You got canapés?

BLAINE. *(Offstage)* On the table.

SARA. *(Examines the tree)* Your tree's too small. And dried out.

BLAINE. *(Offstage)* Gillian fixed it for Boo.

SARA. That explains the color clashes and that avalanche of tinsel. Is everything in metallic this year?

BLAINE. *(Offstage)* The better for Boo to see it.

SARA. Cute. I suppose a little frivolity is good for the soul.

BLAINE. *(Pokes his head in)* The ornaments are gold babies. Hang one.

SARA. You do it. I hate fun. We have three parties tonight. You? Medicine's still a social art. Now they don't allow smoking at Touro, so half of the hospital is chatting on the roof. Glad to see your grades are improving.

BLAINE. *(Offstage)* Solid honors.

SARA. Your father was first of his class.

BLAINE. *(Pokes his head out the door)* I gave up trying to be first. Too much stress on my family.

SARA. Francois runs around catering to everybody. *(Calls out)* Your house is a perpetual mess. Dust can't be good for the baby. How often does your wife clean? Hmph. The word maintenance isn't in Gillian's vocabulary....I have a man general clean our house. It's easier for me to ask a man to do something. For some reason it's always appealed to me. You want his name?

(When BLAINE doesn't respond she screams) Caviar's soggy. *(Calls out to the street)* Francois. *(To BLAINE)* Thinks you are on Saint Anne. He's none of the bad qualities usually associated with social climbers.

(BLAINE enters dressed in a red sweater, fresh shirt, and slacks. He carries a silver pitcher of egg nog and cups.)

BLAINE. I'm glad y'all are happy. Egg nog's nice and hot.

SARA. Good, because your cheese straws are limp. *(Checks her watch)* Where is Gillian? I know this is a snobbish comment. But no woman in the Garden District would keep an in-law waiting. It would never happen. *(Waves to the street)* Francois! Will you come up here. He couldn't find a spot so he's waiting in the car. The category is gone for what Francois does. A true gentleman.

(GILLIAN and DALE enter, dressed in matching long velvet dresses. DALE acts alert, but fragile.)

GILLIAN. My dream is to belt out a slightly bawdy song in a low-cut dress.

SARA. I didn't see you.

DALE. We came through...the back.

GILLIAN. I spent hundreds on a seamstress. Matching dresses in Dale's design.
BLAINE. *(Opens his arms to* **DALE***)* For your first visit home.

DALE. I've got to...be back...by eight o'clock. *(Points to the dresses)* They're not too expensive.

BLAINE. Have I ever denied y'all anything?

DALE. *(Glancing about)* Things look...so bright...and tin...sel...ly.

BLAINE. Sit here, girls. I don't want y'all to get a draft.

SARA. *(To* **GILLIAN***)* What do you do to make men dote on you so?

BLAINE. She exists. *(Puts out some mistletoe and kisses* **GILLIAN***)* Mistletoe.

SARA. Dale, precious, come give me a hug.

BLAINE. *(To* **DALE***)* You look splendid. You've gained weight. Your skin's shiny.

DALE. Is it? I...used that new makeup you sent...Blaine, people at the hospital...make me feel good about myself.

SARA. Don't talk about it.

DALE. I was lost somewhere inside my bad thoughts...but I'm learning how to hold my feelings in check.

GILLIAN. That's great.

BLAINE. Wonderful.

DALE. I've been doing...well in workshop. I drew...some baby clothes...for Blaine, Jr.

GILLIAN. Marvelous.

BLAINE. They're fantastic.

SARA. Yes. The sketches are quite good.

DALE. I'm so breathy...about them. I...designed...a series...for each...month.

GILLIAN. *(Lifting a design. Doorbell rings.)* How adorable.

SARA. *(Rummages in her purse)* Where did I put those clippings from *Le Monde*? Big purses. You can find everything and nothing in them at the same time. *(To* **BLAINE***)* Look at Dale's drawing. Francois thinks one day she'll go to the *École des Beaux Arts*.

(SOUND: The doorbell rings.)

SARA. That's Francois. Tell him I'll be coming along.

BLAINE. You just got here.

SARA. We're on our way to the country club. That's the thing about New Orleans. There're too many parties. Other places, you eat and drink between Thanksgiving and Christmas, then you have a break. Not here, you go right into Mardi Gras, Easter, Saint Patty's day and the Fourth of July. Maybe you should wake the baby so Dale can say goodbye.

DALE. I don't want...Francois...to drive me back. I want Blaine to take me.

SARA. *(Gestures to the rain)* But there's no reason for Blaine to brave this...sleaze. We have to pass the clinic—

BLAINE. I want to drive her. We could look at the Christmas lights. I'll drive you later.

SARA. What a darling boy.

DALE. It's not...too...much...trouble?

BLAINE. 'Course not.

DALE. Thanks.

(Doorbell rings again. **DALE** *exits to the front door.)*

SARA. I don't know if you realize what a darling boy Blaine is. He's a regular Louisiana gentleman. If I could've had sons like Blaine, I would have peopled Louisiana. *(Hands him a money envelope)* Merry Christmas early. I've commissioned a painting of Boo. I detest portraits. Nevertheless we must have them. A good portrait is one of the niceties of civilization. Portraits, and lockets, and silver baby cups. *(*DALE *returns)*

DALE. Oh, you put out...my drawings. And I...love the...tree. With gold...babies.

GILLIAN. Time to put the angel on top.

BLAINE. *(Lifting* **DALE***)* You do it.

SARA. *(To* **BLAINE***)* Don't drop her.

BLAINE. Geez, you're heavy.

SARA. You'll muss her dress.

DALE. The angel's...smiling...on our family.

GILLIAN. Let's turn on Christmas music and get a picture. *(Puts on music)*

SARA. I'll take it. I've a horror of photographs.

GILLIAN. Everybody smile and squish together.

DALE. *(To* **BLAINE***)* Get in the middle.

SARA. A wife, a sister, and a new baby. That's rough.

BLAINE. Should be a banner year.

(The camera flashes, Christmas music like, "Have yourself a Very Merry Chirstmas," plays as the curtain falls.)

(curtain)

APPENDIX

Replace Act One / Scene 4 with scene below that includes a cast of 8 girl MARDI GRAS REVELERS

ACT ONE

Scene Four

(Two months later. Early March, Mardi Gras time. The living room is strewn with **DALE** *'S objects and Mardi Gras decorations and costumes.* **SARA** *enters in a long coat and is talking into a cellular phone. SHE walks before the set as if down a street.)*

SARA. Blaise. Are you there? Pick up...No, I don't want to leave a message so you can wave my laundry over the Quarter. I'll call back. *(Hangs up and dials again)* This is your aunt. Remember? The one who is financing your education. I don't like the role, but I've got to play it. Pick up. *(Slams the phone and dials again)* Blaise, I know you're there. Medical school's over, and it's five-thirty. I got your exam grades. Need I say, I'm horrified. I don't want to be hectored by F reports showing up in my mailbox. When I said medicine was a social art, I didn't mean it was a party. You have my brother's reputation to consider. *(Coughs)* I know the roots of stupidity are complex, but I want you to get your brains and life out of hock. Learning is a slow system of osmosis. Eavesdrop on the smart fellows. Write a longer paper. And please do brown-nose your teachers after class. *(Coughs)* Remember the golden rule. She who has the gold rules. I'm not financing a failure.

(Blackout. Toward the end of **SARA** *'s speech,* **DALE** *enters in a sorcerer's costume with her astrology chart. She is followed by eight girl* **REVELERS***, in grotesque carnival costumes.)*

(The **REVELERS** *dance with homemade instruments and whistle, playing drums, hitting spoons, singing)*

REVELERS. "All because it's carnival time, it's carnival time, it's carnival time, everybody's drinking wine..." Oh, oh you know what it's about time to do. We're going to--Everybody put your hands together. We're going to take you to a Mardi Gras parade.

(Girls clap hands and whistle, dance and sing a Mardi Gras song like, I'm Going to New Orleans *or* When the Saints Go Marching In.*)*

(MUSIC: trumpets, brass. **REVELERS** *do a second line dance back and forth to the balcony)*

*(***GILLIAN** *enters, goes to a corner to rehearse her nurse's role in the television series.* **BLAISE** *follows, going to another part of the room, studying.)*

GILLIAN. Who are those people?

> **DALE.** Friends. They are using our balcony to watch the—
>
> **GILLIAN.** How long will they stay—

DALE. Till the parade passes! *(To* **GILLIAN***)* You're so...so rude!

*(***DALE** *motions the* **REVELERS** *over by* **BLAISE** *and lifts her chart)*

DALE. Blaise has the most wonderful astrology chart.

REVELER #1. There's so much creative giftedness around him--

REVELER #2. *(Continuing thought)* --I've been inhaling.

GILLIAN. *(Calls out)* Ssh. I'm working on my lines.

DALE. Still?

REVELER #3. You have to make art --

REVELER #4. --as if you had eternity.

GILLIAN. *(Studies her script)* "The doctor will be making rounds in a half an hour if you'd like to freshen up."

BLAISE. *(Puts headsets to his ears and opens a book)* I'm going under. Do you know the Australian box jellyfish is the most poisonous one alive? Toxins, that's the theme of the night.

DALE. *(To* **REVELERS***)* Look. I did a watercolor of Blaise's sun sign.

REVELER #5. Maybe finished, maybe not.

REVELER #7. Blaise's an old soul.

REVELER #8. He's had twenty-five hundred lives.

GILLIAN. Get that out of his face. Go outside.

BLAISE. *(Rises)* Come on, girls! *(To* **REVELERS***)* Y'all will have to leave right after the parade.

*(***BLAISE** *shows the* **REVELERS** *to the balcony. Noises from street.* **DALE** *waves the chart in* **GILLIAN***'s face.)*

DALE. Mama studied at the *École des Beaux Arts*, and lived on Beethoven Street—in Paris.

GILLIAN. *(Ignoring her)* "What are these pills doing on the table. You were supposed to take them—"

DALE. Across from the Eiffel Tower. Her apartment once belonged to a Cavalier poet from the seventeenth century.

DALE. "Gather rosebuds while you may and while you're young go marry, for having once lost your prime, you may forever tarry."

GILLIAN. *(Reciting her lines)* Where was I? Oh yes. "You were supposed to take them with your milk—"

DALE. *(To* **GILLIAN***)* Do you want me to do your chart?

REVELERS. *(From balcony)* Throw me something mister!

GILLIAN. Quiet!! I need to concentrate.

REVELERS. *(From balcony)* Hey mister! Mister up here!

GILLIAN. *(Grabs stomach)* Ugh. I've got these awful cramps.

DALE. *(To* **GILLIAN***)* You want a heating pad?

GILLIAN. Get away.

DALE. *(To* **GILLIAN***)* Something to drink? A Coke?—

*(***BLAISE** *returns. Tries to distract* **DALE** *with his textbook)*

BLAISE. Here, sugar. Did you know the cure for a jellyfish is to pour vinegar on the tentacles? Don't pull them off because they release the poison. A brown recluse spider bites you, it can kill you. See the fiddle on its back? A black widow, you spot that, you better squash it.

DALE. Oh. No. Stop. *(Crying)* I'm an Aquarius. We're the sign of the most emotion. I feel for others you see. I believe in non-injury to living things so they can roam free.

REVELERS O.S. Hey throw us some beads. Up here!

GILLIAN. *(Puts in ear plugs)* Time for ear plugs. Where was I ? "Supposed to take them with your milk after breakfast—"

(Police whistles. Sirens getting louder)

REVELERS O.S. Parades coming! Hoo-ray! Hoo-ray!

DALE. *(To* **BLAISE***)* Take a break.

BLAISE. I've got exams the Monday after Mardi Gras—

DALE. I'll quiz you --. On ways to die from poison.

BLAISE. I've got those big tests coming up!

REVELERS. *(Poking in)* Parade's here y'all!!

DALE. *(To* **REVELERS***)* We're not watching! *(To* **BLAISE***, intimately)* Oh look at your chart? Astrology shows you the potential genius of yourself. I'm Aquarius with a moon in Virgo, and you're Virgo with a moon in Pisces.

GILLIAN. Quiet—

DALE. Your horoscope is...a "fortunate" chart.

REVELERS O.S. Throw us something!

GILLIAN. *(Memorizing)* "After your breakfast." No. "After your lunch."

DALE. *(To* **BLAISE***)* You'll always be able to get whatever money you need, and you'll be protected from the worst life can throw at you. For you have the sun in Virgo and the moon in Pisces. Johann Wolfgang von Goethe, born in 1749, had the sun in Virgo and Count Tolstoy, born in 1828, had the moon in Pisces. Moon in Pisces means the aim of your life is to be in tune with the infinite.

GILLIAN. She puts me in a state—

DALE. Something of the magician hovers about you.

GILLIAN. With. . .strangers, useless banter.

DALE. *(To* **BLAISE***)* For you've a guardian angel, at your side. And she will give you the power over the world that the Magic Lamp gave to Aladdin.

(Sirens blare outside as a parade approaches. Throughout the sequence music blasts in from the street)

REVELERS O.S. It's coming! It's coming!

GILLIAN. Shut up! *(Rising)* Get rid of...those...those freaks! Weirdos! Tramps!

DALE. You ruined my reading...I have no friends...you--

GILLIAN. Blaise, do something.

BLAISE. It's so exhausting—

DALE. *(To* **GILLIAN***)* Go to your room.

BLAISE. To have to be an evangelist.

DALE. Witch.

GILLIAN. She's off on a rage again.

DALE. Gillian's so mean.

GILLIAN. You hear her, Blaise?

BLAISE. *(Packing his books)* I'm looking for quiet.

GILLIAN. When I've suffered the—
BLAISE. The quiet I can't get.

REVELERS O.S. *(singing)* Hey!! Hey rock and roll!!

GILLIAN. *(Pointing toward REVELERS)* The degradation of strangers...a sister-in-law who's a...a--

REVELERS O.S. *(singing)* Hey!! Hey rock and roll!!

GILLIAN. Oh, my stomach hurts. Your sister's constantly misbehaving a worthless—Restless anxious—being—Oh, my stomach hurts so bad. Ah. Oh.

(REVELERS enter with handkerchiefs and napkins doing a second line.)

ALL REVELERS. We're about to do the indoor second line.

REVELER #7. *(Explaining to GILLIAN)* The second line is a dance we do in New Orleans--

REVELER #8. Whenever there is a reason to celebrate.

GILLIAN. My period's so screwed up.

BLAISE. Lie down.

DALE. She wants attention.

REVELER #2. You wave that handkerchief in the air--

GILLIAN. Oh. These cramps.

BLAISE. Is that blood?

REVELER #4. Get on up.

GILLIAN. God. Help me.

REVELER #5 and #6. *(Screams)* Talking about hey--

BLAISE. Get a towel.

DALE. Where?

BLAISE. Towel!!

REVELERS #2 and #1. *(Chanting)* Aiko aiko one day.

BLAISE. There. Call an ambulance.

DALE. Streets are roped off.

REVELERS #3, #4, #5. *(Chanting)* Cha qua mo cha qua mo fille anne.

GILLIAN. I can't stop the bleeding.

REVELERS #6, #7, #8. Feel that music I been told. It's good for your body and good for your soul...

BLAISE. A damn ambulance.

REVELERS. Now everybody say, I done got over...Everybody sing! Hey. Hey. Hey. Hey Hey Hey. Hey Hey Hey Hey--

*(A band blares outside as **REVELERS** dance. **DALE** runs toward the balcony)*

DALE. Parade's here!

*(**DALE** is on balcony. **BLAISE** hovers over **GILLIAN** and **REVELERS** take over singing as lights fade.)*

(blackout)

Also by Rosary Hartel O'Neill...

The Awakening of Kate Chopin

Black Jack: The Thief of Possession

Degas in New Orleans

John Singer Sargent and Madame X

Marilyn/God

Property

Solitaire

Turtle Soup

Uncle Victor

White Suits in Summer

The Wings of Madness

Wishing Aces

Please visit our website **samuelfrench.com** for complete descriptions and licensing information.

OTHER TITLES AVAILABLE FROM SAMUEL FRENCH

PROPERTY

Rosary Hartel O'Neill

Full Length, Southern Comedy / 2m, 3f / Unit set

Property is a contemporary romantic comedy set in a Garden District mansion in New Orleans. Rooster Dubonnet, a young artist suffering from a terminal disease, is dazzled by love. Raised by an imperious society-driven mother, he has fallen in love with a New-Age nurse. Set during Mardi Gras–when a whole tradition of fun, revelry, and prestige seizes the city– Rooster is caught between his dedication to his family's past (and "property") and his own very different future.

SAMUELFRENCH.COM

OTHER TITLES AVAILABLE FROM SAMUEL FRENCH

SOLITAIRE

Rosary Hartel O'Neill

Full Length, Southern Comedy / 3m, 2f / Interior

The Mississippi Gulf Coast estate of Irene Dubbonet is an unforgetable place to visit, but who would want to live there? All of her relatives, who hope to inherit it! This is a play about manipulation and what happens to family members' dreams when the odds are stacked against them. A cloud of doom hangs over Serenity Manor, until at last, virtue triumphs. Irene's son, the artist, Rooster, deeply anxious to prove himself, connives a scheme to help his "down and out" brother-in-law seize the estate. Funny situations sparked by witty lines bring the audience into an intriguing overview of topsy-turvy privileged life today.

SAMUELFRENCH.COM

OTHER TITLES AVAILABLE FROM SAMUEL FRENCH

DEGAS IN NEW ORLEANS

Rosary Hartel O'Neill

Full Length, Drama / 3m, 6f / One integrated int/ext set.

A historical drama that explores Edgar Degas' scandalous visit to New Orleans in 1872. Edgar Degas, the French Impressionist painter, is torn between helping his relatives in America and pursuing a career as a painter. Fame and family obligations come to a head when he discovers he is still in love with his sister-in-law, who is now pregnant and blind. As Edgar struggles with his own ethical conundrum, he discovers that his aggressively charming brother has gone through all the family money in an attempt to save his uncle's sugar business.

SAMUELFRENCH.COM

www.ingramcontent.com/pod-product-compliance
Lightning Source LLC
Chambersburg PA
CBHW070646300426
44111CB00013B/2292